IN SEARCH OF THE MISSING ELEPHANT

Selected Essays by Donald N. Michael

With an Introduction by Graham Leicester

D0493871

An International Futures Forum Publication

International Futures Forum

The Boathouse
Silversands
Hawkcraig Road
Aberdour
Fife KY3 0TZ
Scotland
Tel +44 (0)1383 861300
www.internationalfuturesforum.com

Published in this edition in 2010 by:

Triarchy Press
Station Offices
Axminster
Devon. EX13 5PF
United Kingdom
+44 (0)1297 631456
info@triarchypress.com
www.triarchypress.com

tp

A catalogue record for this book is available from the British Library.

Cover design and all artwork by Heather Fallows -
www.whitespacegallery.org.uk

ISBN: 978-0-9562631-8-6

CONTENTS

INTRODUCTION

Don Michael was a remarkable man whose writings about the condition of humanity in the face of an uncertain future ring with clarity and wisdom to this day.

Yet they are little known and difficult to come by. His one great book, *On Learning to Plan—and Planning to Learn,* written when he was 50, is full of insight, but not an easy read. And the rest of his thoughts are scattered through diverse journal articles, texts and speeches. He was a reluctant writer, as his friend Ed Schein observed, because 'he didn't like to formalize' and was always conscious of the dangers of over-simplification.

His later essays, the fruits of the period after he left the University of Michigan to enjoy an active 'retirement' in San Francisco, are gems of clarity, pungent with the wisdom of experience. Four of those essays are reprinted here, including his last published work—the address he gave on receiving an honorary degree from Saybrook Graduate School which gives this book its title. One earlier essay is also included from 1973, the same year as *On Learning to Plan*—to provide some continuity with the earlier period of his professional life.

I hope these fragments will encourage readers both to explore more of Don's writing, and to continue the work he began (as I hope the International Futures Forum is doing).

With that in mind, this introduction both outlines my own discovery of Don's writing, and places the five essays included here in the wider context of his life and work.

First Encounter

I came to Don Michael through his friends. In December 2000, shortly after Don died, I issued an invitation to a group of remarkable individuals to participate in an initiative

I was just launching, the International Futures Forum. This is what it said:

> 'In the early eighteenth century in Scotland there emerged a cluster of philosophers, social scientists, moralists and others who together helped to shape what came to be known as the enlightenment. They explored the assumptions, values and principles of the move from a pre-industrial to an industrial age, the rise of secularism and reason.

> 'Those assumptions, values and principles of the enlightenment are today under strain. We live in a new, networked economy in which the old rules are being subverted. The political institutions bequeathed to us by the eighteenth century are suffering a twin crisis of legitimacy and competence. The legacy of the invisible hand is a combination of threats to our ecosystem that endanger our survival. And the triumph of reason and of modern science has left us alienated from the life of the spirit, searching for meaning.

> 'It seems appropriate then that a second cluster of individuals should emerge in Scotland seeking to reinvent the spirit of the enlightenment: to explore the assumptions, values and underpinning principles of today's transition—beyond the industrial society.

> 'In St Andrews in April 2001 we will inaugurate the International Futures Forum (IFF). This is a dialogue centred on a group of leading strategic thinkers brought together to explore the nature of the most significant future challenges facing society and the systemic connections between them; to examine ways in which we might successfully adapt and respond to these challenges, including by learning from existing promising practice; and to stimulate actions consonant with that inquiry by individual communities and at a systemic level, in Scotland and elsewhere.'

We structured the dialogue around four domains in which the challenge of adaptation to a changing world seemed most fundamental: governance, sustainability, consciousness and economy.

My invitation was sent to a selection of individuals around the world who could contribute on any or all of those themes. It turned out that they included a number of people who had known Don Michael.

Just before our first IFF meeting in St Andrews in April 2001 one of these people sent me a short paper he suggested 'might be of interest to other participants'. It was Michael Marien's memorial Future Survey collection of abstracts from some of Don's later work.[1] It ran from 'Competence and Compassion in an Age of Uncertainty' (1983) to 'Some Observations with regard to a Missing Elephant' (Winter 2000).

I lighted on the Missing Elephant paper in particular as gold dust. Here was a man articulating just what I felt about the world—so boundlessly complex, radically interconnected and fast-changing that we are no longer able to make sense of it and therefore struggle to take effective action.

I realised that Don had imagined the IFF project long before I had... and was grateful that his friends were able to contribute some of his wisdom. His image of the missing elephant has become a part of IFF mythology—and graces the frontispiece of *Ten Things to do in a Conceptual Emergency* (the book arising from IFF's work first published in 2003).

I later came to read Don's great book *On Learning to Plan—and Planning to Learn*.[2] It is a treasure trove of references to fascinating material—quite apart from the thesis Don develops himself through the book. I was struck by one particular insight that has shaped the way I see the world today:

> *'One of the functions organizations perform is to buffer the individual member from the impact of the chaotic interrelation of everything to everything. Ideally organizations free the member to deal with just so much of the environment as his intellect and psyche permit'.*

In other words, our organisations are there to provide a zone of competence—to keep the 'blooming, buzzing confusion' outside the door at bay. Don's point is that the confusion is too great today to allow that approach. We have to engage with the world as it is. But few of us are up for the struggle.

That for me goes to the heart of the book and of Don's work: the honesty and insight about *resistance* to learning. Our inevitable tendency to deny uncertainty as a means of maintaining psychological security.

This is the leitmotif of Don's writings: the constant tension between the pressing need to learn and the obstacles to learning.

That tension is summed up in a poignant phrase from the Missing Elephant:

> *'One hopes that one can make a difference in the face of all that stands in the way of making a difference.'*

The essays reprinted here are part of a deep and thoughtful commentary on that single question: how to make a difference in the face of all that stands in the way of making a difference?

Don Michael's Professional Life

To gain the most from these writings it is instructive to consider them in the context of Don's evolving life's work. Since his writing can be both timeless and prescient in turns, it is easy to forget that it was the product of a specific time and place and the trajectory of a single life.

This brief biography is taken from one of Don's early essays on 'Space Exploration and the Values of Man' published in the early 1960s:[3]

> 'Donald N Michael was born in Chicago in 1923. He received his bachelor of science degree, in physics, from Harvard University; his Masters of Arts degree from the University of Chicago; and his doctorate from Harvard University in social psychology. From 1944 to 1946 he was an electronics engineer with the US army Signal Corps and worked on radar and signal communications developments. He has been an adviser to the Joint Chiefs of Staff of the Department of Defense and to the National Science Foundation. He is presently a senior research associate for Dunlap and Associates, conducting man-machine systems analysis studies for large weapons systems.'

Later he moved on to work with the Brookings Institution and the Peace Research Institute.

Then in 1967 he left Washington and the world of politics and policy-making to join the University of Michigan—as Professor of Planning and Public Policy and Professor of Psychology. He retired from those roles in 1981, moving to San Francisco—where he seems to have lived a simple, frugal life outside any institution and identified only as 'Professor Emeritus from the University of Michigan'... but still writing and publishing, talking, learning, participating in projects, lecturing, supporting friends.

I wonder what this trajectory has to tell us about where a concerned, compassionate, intelligent, individual committed to public service and social learning can find to stand in the world? I assume that Don left Washington because the politics turned sour after Kennedy and the shift to Nixon. I wonder what influence Don subsequently found in the Academy? Certainly his post-retirement papers, including those reprinted in this volume, are the most engaging and broad and challenging. Perhaps one can only express oneself so clearly when free from institutional constraints?

But there may also be a price to pay in being outside the charmed circle. In *On Learning to Plan* Don uses the notion of 'ideas in good currency'. Where does one have to stand in order to have one's ideas be in good currency? What is the relationship between what you have to say, and where you stand to say it? And how much does that matter in the small matter of 'making a difference'?

Early Work

Don's early writings during the 1950s were inevitably coloured by the pervasive fears of the time. So we find this humble, compassionate man making himself useful by writing on such subjects as 'Civilian Behavior Under Atomic Bombardment' or 'Psychological Effects on Ground Force Troops in Combat of Exposure to Atomic Attack'. Those titles perhaps help to explain Don's lifelong attention to the shadow side of humanity's 'progress'.

But he was also fascinated and excited by the possibilities of technology. He wrote about this in *Cybernation*, published in 1962[4]—a book that was a notable popular success and helped establish Don's reputation as one of the first 'futurists' (a word he hated). In this book we catch a first glimpse of the missing elephant—at this stage well in view, and ready to be corralled by the wonders of data processing:

*'Management in business or government can have much
better control both over the system as it operates and over the
introduction of changes into future operations. Indeed, the
changes themselves may be planned in conformity with, and
guided by, a strategy that is derived from computer analysis of
the future environment'.*

The interest in *planning* the future is clear. Yet already
he sounds darker warnings. The fate of those of us unable
to keep up with information overload and therefore reliant
on government and others to tell us what is true; the
alienation between government and the governed as a result;
depersonalisation in a data-rich environment of control;
the angst and ennui of having nothing to do, deprived of the
dignity and identity of work.

It is his writing about space exploration at this time that
really intrigues me. Ed Schein recalls that when he met
Don at Harvard in the social relations department he clearly
wanted to be a physicist and really wanted to study science.
He was fascinated with the race into space and even—so Ed
tells us—bought a ticket for a flight to the moon. But this
was far more than a fascination with technological advance
or computing power. Through these essays Don begins
to express a deeper story—notably in his piece on 'Space
Exploration and the Values of Man'.

It is clear from this essay that on one level Don saw the
space programme simply as new subject matter for some old,
ingrained patterns of behaviour:

*'What it does is deepen old ruts for the most part rather than
break new pathways. And for leadership space provides a
sharpened axe and many more backs to bury it in.'*

On a psychological level, he asks whether we are going
into space to 'indulge in the primitive fantasy wishes of
children that somewhere there is a good fairy who will make
everything right'. Don knows there is no good fairy: just by
escaping the Earth man will not also escape 'Earth's present

and continuing problems, conflicts of interest, man's battle within himself'.

> *'To build a society of enlightened citizens is a far more monumental task' he says, 'than building a colony on Mars. To build such a society requires an understanding of the behavior of men and an application of that understanding to the improvement of society.... The inward frontiers are as challenging, as dangerous, as rewarding, and as fraught with social significance as any of those beyond earth.'*

There is an energy and a dynamism in this vision. As there is in Don's writing on the technologically enabled 'Cybernation'. He sees his role as raising awareness of 'sometimes acutely uncomfortable aspects... with which we must successfully contend' in order to realise the benefits of such progress.

I see *On Learning to Plan—and Planning to Learn* as the culmination of this phase of Don's career. It is neither an optimistic nor a pessimistic book. It is more a technical volume. It embodies a faith in the future, a faith in planning and a faith in our personal and institutional capacity to learn—to contend successfully with the 'uncomfortable aspects' of our designs. It was published when Don was 50. It seems in retrospect less a culmination and more a staging post at the mid-point of his career.

At the Crossroads

FROM this point on, at least to my ear, the tone becomes more gloomy. In truth that tone is always present. If *On Learning to Plan* is a plea for what society needs, it is accompanied always by a recognition that society is unlikely to listen or respond.

The first essay reprinted here and published at about the same time, in 1973, starkly picks up on this bleak tone: 'Technology and the Management of Change from the

Perspective of a Culture Context'. In terms of the trajectory of Don's thinking over time, this essay feels like a crossroads.

The theme is the challenge of making sense of a complex, human world. It describes a 'turbulent' social environment, full of secondary and tertiary effects from multiple interactions. Don laments the absence of data about how people actually behave in social and institutional settings (rather than abstract data from computer modelling).

He is beginning to reveal his disquiet with the inadequacies of a model of understanding that assumes both systemic knowledge of the whole system and real knowledge about how human beings behave. In practice we do not possess such knowledge, so any model must be misleading or at least inadequate. His conclusion, which becomes a familiar refrain in Don's work from this point on, is that 'we literally do not know what we are talking about much of the time'.

 He notes again how 'putting a man on the moon' is a relatively simple, technical task—not to be compared with the far more difficult task of intervening in social reality to *develop a society and institutions in which man may be allowed to reach his full capacities'.*

He longs for 'disruptable' organisational structures, able to respond to a rapidly changing environment—but notes that 'short of catastrophe and deep crisis, the tendency is to cling to rigid unresponding structures'. He wants our politics to be error-embracing, long range and open to learning rather than short-termist and peddling false certainty. But he cannot see it happening: '...how these needs might be reconciled is completely unknown at this time'.

He paints a bleak vision of the future for the US:

> *'All evidence suggests that, at least for the next couple of decades, the United States will be a highly turbulent society more likely than not, demoralizing itself into a splintered, culturally amorphous state of chronic social crises and catastrophe... All*

> *traditional [governance] approaches are likely to be relatively inadequate, and all new approaches are likely to have a high rate of failures as would any experiments performed under such relatively blind and complicated conditions.... We need to acknowledge that, somehow, we have discovered and are ensnared in a new wilderness, a new jungle, and that the skills that got us here are inadequate to get us out. Looking around us, we must acknowledge that we really are lost.'*

It is the first cry of real despair.

But characteristically it also contains a scintilla of that vital ingredient—hope:

> *'There is to my mind a slight hope—but only a slight hope— that with luck and wisdom and deliberate research we will learn enough about the appropriate culture base for such a society to be able to establish the conditions for managing a society of this complexity... To ask what these values and procedures would be and when they will be in operation would be much like asking members of feudal culture to characterize the yet-to-be-evolved culture based on a money and market economy. They simply couldn't do so: the experiences upon which to base the concepts didn't exist'.*

So can we do it? Will we find the right combination of luck, wisdom and deliberate research to find a way of managing today's complex society? Can we find our way through?

> *'I doubt it, but none of us understands the dynamics of societies well enough to be sure. So I shall continue to try.'*

Continuing to Try

THE journey recorded in Don's articles published after he left academia and moved to San Francisco is more reflective and more concerned with a meta-level analysis. He is no longer writing about technology, or space travel, or young people, or social policy. Instead his writing becomes — for me at least — more explicitly about processes of social change and resistance: social learning.

The theme of governance comes to the fore. And the theme of futures thinking also becomes more explicit, perhaps as a result of his connection with Global Business Network, then in its infancy. But the theme that runs through all of these writings is psychological incoherence and a feeling of conceptual rootlessness. These pieces are all about aspects of the conceptual emergency.

The second essay in this volume, 'Forecasting and Planning in an Incoherent Context', published in 1989, is particularly dark. Don argues that forecasting and planning require a coherent context. But there are fundamental epistemological, social and psychodynamic incoherences in the contemporary context that are impossible either to ignore or to repress.

Planning and forecasting in the traditional sense are useless in such an environment, but:

> *'the pressures for short term responses to critical issues will increase and, given the incoherences, dominate social action. The presence of forecasts and planning efforts will further complicate the context, if they have much effect at all.'*

There is a first stirring of the missing elephant thesis — a herd of elephants:

> *'The more complexity plus more inevitably incomplete information about the human condition encourages selecting from these multiple, confusing and uncertain signals those most compatible with one's preferred ways of perceiving and evaluating the world. The number of blind persons and the number of elephants subject to interpretation increase.'*

The abstract is pithy:

'All of us are sinking in this ontological and epistemological swamp. To paraphrase the Tao Te Ching: those who know can not say; those who say do not know. So be it.'

He is clear-eyed and courageous in detailing in this essay the depths of our ignorance.

We have no adequate **theory**:

'If human activity is describable as sequences of causes and effects in the way other processes seem to be, we are a very long way from any theory of social or individual change under turbulent conditions.'

The theory must relate observed micro-behaviour and experience with greater social phenomena at the macro level. He points to the theory of 'emergence' as promising:

'I subscribe to Polanyi's argument that creative human activities have an 'emergent' quality: the whole is unpredictably greater than the sum of the parts.'

But even if such a theory is developed, it still cannot be assumed to have much predictive power:

'Humans experiencing chaotic processes through the peephole of their consciousness and the depths of their unconsciousness cannot act towards those chaotic circumstances as they would if they were merely observing them from outside. They/we live in them and are not about to wait out the painful and problematic transformations'.

We are struggling too for coherence in **governance**:

'Not only do we lack concepts of governance appropriate for guiding an increasingly interconnected world, but more to the point we lack concepts appropriate during the period of incoherence, with its attendant turbulence and disruption, during the transition from now to whatever and whenever more coherent forms might emerge.'

And the causes of the struggle go deeper still:

> 'Underlying these difficulties is the deeper incoherence—what values should determine the appropriate location of system boundaries? There is no operating system of shared values that presumes a both/and, interactive, interdependent human condition. Instead survival of the fittest contends with being thy sibling's keeper. As Macintyre has demonstrated, all we possess are remnants of previously demolished value systems.'

And there is a core concern with the quality of **education**.

Don from the start took a great interest in the lives of young people and adolescents. When he imagined the future he imagined their future—usually no more than 20 years ahead. In this essay he laments the capacity of teachers and parents—what he calls 'the culture bearers'—to shape:

> 'a next generation able to grow into emotionally mature, cognitively competent, and socially responsible adults, essential for maintaining a complex and humane world'. But for the most part adults are 'mostly unable or unwilling to think with the subtlety, skill, and persistence required for critical rather than ritual participation in the conduct of governance that seeks to overcome the conditions described here'.

And they lack what we in IFF have come to call 'psychological literacy'—or 'psychological capacity':

> 'at least an understanding and feeling for the basics of psychodynamics as they affect one's own behavior and that of others in the public arena. But of course no such educational goals or child-rearing norms exist in society at large, if for no other reason than the traditional myths that guide Western societies (and most others) do not require such competencies of their members. They really have not been necessary until recent times'.

The Practice of Futures Thinking

TYPICALLY Don did not absolve himself and his colleagues from the responsibility to reflect on their practice in this incoherent world. The third essay reprinted here 'With Both Feet Planted Firmly in Mid-Air: reflections on thinking about the future' (1985) is particularly incisive.

Don warns us to be alert to the psychological needs—in both clients and practitioners—that futures thinking can pander to. Commissioning a big futures study, for example, can play to an organisation's existing myth of control:

> *'That the consumer of futures studies is able to commandeer the combined resources of logic and expertise itself engenders a comforting sense of being in control thereby reducing anxiety about the unknown future.'*

There are psychological rewards too for futures practitioners in undertaking such prestigious—and expensive—projects:

> *'Taking part encourages the belief that one is influential, making a difference, being socially potent and powerful... While his or her work is underway, I have yet to meet a 'futurist' who didn't feel socially significant and personally vitalized by visions of potential effect amplified by the perceived status of the study commissioners.'*

But how can we take these factors into account? In an earlier essay on denial—'Reason's Shadow'[5]—Don reached a typically tentative conclusion about the capacity to include extra-rational, emotional and psychological aspects in sense-making and policy-making:

> *'Will it matter that we add to our concerns the contribution of unconscious forces and directives? As with all else we face in this uncertain, turbulent, poorly understood, and occasionally rational world, we shall have to learn whether it matters by what happens when we do add this ingredient to the stew of ideas and reason. And we shall have to learn, too, how to add*

this ingredient so that it blends with the others rather than destroys the dish. This is exotic stuff!'

But while his essay on thinking about the future claims to be about epistemology—what are we thinking about when we think about the future, and what are we willing to include as data?—at its core is a thesis about ethics.

Don quotes Seymour Sarson, as he often does, on the more positive aspects of our deeper unconscious drives:

'Emotions are critical to what happens—both those emotions driving creativity and reason, aspiration, power, greed and the will to control; and those emotions struggling with the existential questions of being human. As Seymour Sarson summarizes them, they are: how to dilute the individual's sense of aloneness in the world, how to engender and maintain a sense of community, and how to justify living even though one will die.

'It is not enough to share thoughts about the future restricted to a description of the costs and benefits of introducing one or another new technology, policy or procedure to better realise the intentions of a public or private organization. Somewhere in the process the recipients of the study should be inspired to ask themselves 'what is it all for? Why give thought to the future? Surely not just for profits, or jobs, or the next election or budget hearing. These are very important, of course, but really, what is it all for? Why am I doing what I am?

'We are not outside the story we tell: each of us is part of the story. Each must be a quester after existential meaning, vulnerable, uncertain, and ethically concerned about what happens to our thoughts about the future since, it they are used, they will affect the future we are telling stories about.'

Hope, Anyone?

THIS question of the value of futures thinking and futures studies and the stance of the practitioner as part of the story is taken up in another magnificent essay, written at around the same time and reprinted here: 'Leadership's Shadow: the dilemma of denial'.

It was first given as an address to the Club of Rome on the occasion of its 20th anniversary. It could equally be an address to the IFF on our tenth. It is a thoughtful and candid examination of why the collective efforts of so many well-intentioned, highly intelligent, committed individuals and organisations have made so little impact on the way the world is going.

Characteristically Don includes himself in that number: 'what follows is an argument with myself'—he begins— 'albeit a polemic too'.

> *'The most profound threat to the development of a planetary civilization is the inability of leaders to admit that there are fundamental circumstances with which we must deal that cannot be acknowledged.'*

There are too many taboo areas. And once they become taboos society reinforces the process that keeps them that way: 'As Freud observed, the first thing that is denied is the fact of denial as a pervasive psychological condition.'

Don lists four taboos that are not readily admitted in the world of public discourse and public action (he has a sideswipe at the Club of Rome for being disconnected from both worlds—and therefore more open to discussing the taboos). They will be familiar by now:

- No coherent theory of social change under turbulence. 'It is all bailing wire and Scotch tape. We do not know where we are going.'
- A poorly educated population, due to 'inept child education and parents and teachers passing on to

the next generation the consequences of their own neuroses and counter-productive lifestyles.'

- The denial of the power of unconscious forces, when we know that 'unconsciously driven hopes, fears, obsessions, prejudices, tantrums and habits carry the day in corporate boardrooms, government offices, and wherever else values, goals and personalities clash or mesh'.

- And no ethics. 'We have no ethics, nor do we know what the ethics should be, appropriate for making hard choices in a contentious yet systemic world.' If everything is connected to everything else in time and space, then 'the buck doesn't stop anywhere'.

These taboos are kept in place partly because it is just bad politics to open up these issues in public. But there is also something more fundamental. Ignorance is protective. When confronted with uncomfortable facts it takes considerable psychological strength to shun the comforts of denial:

'It is a rare leader who is thoughtful and knowledgeable enough and who possesses the psychological maturity to look into the abyss.'

Don concludes, as we would expect, that a stance open to learning, personally and socially, is required.

'Such a society would self-consciously question its premises as well as its actions, accept uncertainty, and measure leadership competence at all levels by its capacity to acknowledge ignorance and uncertainty as prerequisites for discovery and change, i.e. as the conditions for learning.'

That—as we know from his previous writing—is a very tall order.

And so we come to the final section of the speech. 'Where does this leave those of us who have trudged this far into the thicket?' asks Don. Gloomy and depressed. And fearful.

> 'I expect the psychological, social and economic costs of the pile-up of interlocked complexities to accelerate. And, as tolerance for these costs evaporates over time, perhaps society will slouch into something quite different and probably very unpleasant, some kind of an updated European 14th century or Japanese 16th and early 17th centuries.'

But we can hope for something better. We cannot be optimistic, but we can hope. The final section of the essay is headed, rather forlornly: 'Hope, anyone?'

> 'Perhaps a combination of tinkering with the surface of things, forced by contending grass roots agitation, illuminated by the critical interpretations of some thinkers, and inspired by occasional enlightened and fortunate leaders, together with the extraordinary adaptability of this species will result in societies more slowly burdened by deepening costs and, therefore, tolerant enough of them to avoid total collapse from conflict and despair.

> 'After all, many in the US population today are subject to terribly difficult lives, but they go on living, making what they can of their circumstances. And there are many innovative social experiments and some probing critical commentary forwarded to counter these degraded conditions, to create more enlightened ways of being and doing.

> 'So there are reasons to hope—not to be optimistic but to hope. In the first place, for humans to stop hoping is to guarantee both individual and societal premature death. Moreover, given our ignorance, we cannot conclude that nothing can be done.

> 'There is no way to know beforehand whether this incremental effort matters. But if we are ever to unravel what I believe to be an ever tightening, self-complicating knot, some of whose lineaments I've tried to discern, it will be necessary (though not sufficient) to bring to bear all the understanding we can by

*acknowledging the intellectual and psychodynamic fix we are
in instead of ignoring them in the name of optimism or positive
vision.'*

The Missing Elephant

So finally we come to the missing elephant, the essay that
first enthralled me. It is elegant in its simplicity—the
simplicity the other side of complexity. The original speech,
given at Saybrook in October 1998 when Don, then in his
70s, received an honorary degree, is very direct. I prefer
it to the official version published later in the *Journal of
Humanistic Psychology* in Winter 2000 when it was 'tidied up'
for an academic audience. The original is more human, more
touching and is included here.

It is not the first time that Don uses the blind men and
the elephant story. Previously he has used it to illustrate the
implication that there is a storyteller—someone who can
see the elephant and the blind men, and can therefore tell
the story from that perspective. His central message this
time around is that the storyteller too is blind. There is no
elephant because nobody has the vision to tell the story.

He recites six causes of the storyteller's blindness, six
'ignorance maintaining characteristics'. They are by now
familiar. And he could have added more.

He appears to suggest that the contemporary operating
environment is just too complex to allow for coherent policy
or action:

*'There is no agreed on interpretation that provides an enduring
basis for coherent action based on an understanding of the
enfolding context.'*

And yet this is not a counsel of despair:

*'I wouldn't be here, accepting an honorary degree from
Saybrook or taking your time, if I believed that what many*

of us are about was futile. Instead I hope to add a deeper appreciation of the existential challenge we face, the poignancy of our efforts, and the admiration they merit as we try to deal with our circumstances.'

It is the simplicity of the eight ways he identifies to *respond* that is beguiling. After all the energy and complexity of the early work, the dark forebodings of the middle period, he seems to reach a serene understanding of what it is that each of us must do to make a difference.

'First be hopeful. Hope not optimism. 'Hope has to do with looking directly at the circumstances we're dealing with; at the challenges we must accept as finite and vulnerable beings and activities; recognizing the limits of our very interpretation of what we're committing ourselves to, and still go on because one hopes that one can make a difference in the face of all that stands in the way of making a difference.

'This means acting according to what I have been calling 'tentative commitment'. That means you are willing to look at the situation carefully enough, to risk enough, to contribute enough effort, to hope enough, to undertake your project. And to recognize, given our vulnerability and finiteness, our ineluctable ignorance, that we may well have it wrong. We may have to back off. We may have to change not only how we're doing it, but doing it at all. And then do so!

'And finally, practise compassion. Given the circumstances I have described, facing life requires all the compassion we can bring to others and to ourselves. Be as self conscious as possible, as much of the time as possible, and thereby recognize that we all live in illusion, we all live in ignorance, we are all struggling to cope with the existential questions of life, death and meaning. And that we all need help facing this reality, help that goes by the name of practising compassion. The blind must care for the blind.'

Graham Leicester 2010

Notes and References

1   'The Don Michael Memorial Convocation', 25 March 2001, special edition of *Future Survey*, editor Michael Marien.

2   Donald N. Michael, *On Learning to Plan—and Planning to Learn*, San Francisco, 1973.

3   Donald N. Michael, 'Space Exploration and the Values of Man', *Space Journal*, 1959.

4   Donald N. Michael, *Cybernation: The Silent Conquest,* Center for the Study of Democratic Institutions, Santa Barbara, California, 1962.

5   Donald N. Michael, 'Reason's Shadow: Notes on the Psychodynamics of Obstruction', *Technological Forecasting and Social Change*, 26, 149-153, 1984.

TECHNOLOGY AND THE MANAGEMENT OF CHANGE FROM THE PERSPECTIVE OF A CULTURE CONTEXT

IF one defines a crucial characteristic of modernization as being an activity that extends into the future, then modernization necessarily becomes a problem in the management of change. But the meaning of management, of change itself, and the context for engineering particular changes either by political means or by those of organizational or individual development, all will depend on the culture characteristics of the society. Of the many culture characteristics that must be attended to in such change management approaches, I will focus here on the relation of technological change to social change as mediated by the culture context. I will emphasize technology because, in the United States, the creation and availability of increasingly complex and powerful technologies have, to the extent we understand social process, contributed enormously to and, until recently, have been reinforced by the particular culture characteristics of that society. Technology is not the only factor that needs be attended to in order to appreciate the nature of the task of managing social change. But, to the extent that modernization is dependent on the availability of technological resources and technological prowess, the ways technology is valued and used may tell us important things about the culture prerequisites for managing social change.

There is in the anthropological literature a continuing debate on the nature of culture and the objective evidence for this abstract concept. Of the definitions and theories that have been argued among anthropologists, certainly those of Clyde Kluckhohn rank among the most influential. Partly because he was my mentor and partly because his definitions are particularly useful for our purposes, I will apply the concept of culture in keeping with his ideas as set out in his chapter, "The Concept of Culture," published, appropriately enough, in *The Science of Man in the World Crisis*.[1] I quote:

"A culture is a historically derived system of explicit and implicit designs for living, which tends to be shared by all or specially designated members of a group, (p. 98.) A culture is not only a reticulum of patterned means for satisfying needs but equally a network of stylized goals for individual and group achievement, (p. 104.) Almost no human situations are viewed in ways which are altogether a consequence of the individual's experience. Culture is-among other things-a set of ready-made definitions of the situation which each participant only slightly retailors in his own idiomatic way. (p. 91.) Cultures create needs as well as provide a means of fulfilling them. (p. 81.) Cultures create problems as well as solving them. (p. 81.) Most specific needs can be satisfied in a wide variety of ways but 'the culture selects' only one or a very few of the organically and physically possible modes. 'The culture selects' is, to be sure, a metaphorical way of speaking. The <u>original</u> choice was necessarily made by an individual and then followed by other individuals (or it wouldn't have become culture). But from the angle of those individuals who later learn this bit of culture the existence of this element in a design for living has the <u>effect</u> of a selection which was not made by these human beings as a reaction to their own particular situation but was rather a choice made by individuals long gone but which still tends to bind our contemporary actors." (p. 95.)

In other words, we are attending to the *patterned* set of values and behaviors that people hold about what is right and worthy and wrong and undesirable, and it is that set of values toward technology and its utility and the expected behaviors expressing those values that we will examine.[2]

Some preliminary comments are in order, however, about the limits of approaching the management of change through the concept of the cultural environment. In the first place, the concept of culture is an abstraction as is the concept of society. These concepts are not precise and their imprecision is made greater by the pervasive lack of useful data about how men actually behave in their social and institutional settings. Such data would permit us to refine these concepts and to judge better their applicability to on-going circumstances. Presently, we simply do not have enough data: we literally do not know what we are talking about much of the time when we claim to be describing and analyzing the behavior of men and institutions either as it has occurred in history or at the present time—to say nothing of the future. In the United States, a growing awareness of the need for social indicator data is evidence of an appreciation developing at the political as well as academic level that, in fact, we do not know what is happening well enough to check which of various theories are appropriate for explaining and predicting what is happening. Not only do we lack data about what is happening now, but we lack data about how the present came to be. That is, we lack longitudinal data that records over time how men effect and are affected by their social and technological environment.

All of these comments hold with particular emphasis when we are trying to understand the role of technology with regard to social changes. Data-based knowledge is prerequisite to the development of appropriate schemes for the management of change particularly in the light of the potentialities and the problems inherent in new technologies. Hence, what I have to say, indeed whatever anyone says, about the relationship of technology to social change is necessarily speculative.

There are many studies which attempt with considerable useful insight to relate one or another set of factors which seem to be of particular pertinence, but I must emphasize that we presently lack the methods and the data for generalizing these interpretations and for projecting them into the future. To be sure, within groups of observers there can be found consensus about what is happening to society. But this is more an indication of how people protect, maintain, and elaborate the vested interests of their subcultures through what they pay attention to than it is evidence of the validity of viewpoints held. And, of course, what is attended to is, to a large degree, culturally determined through the definitions of what particular groups ought to pay attention to. Indeed, it is only with the growth of concerns such as those which are focused on in this conference that time, effort, and approval will be applied in sufficient degree to begin to provide us with a firm foundation for analyzing and forecasting the relationship of technological change to social change in a given cultural context.

Cultural and social change is also a function of the cultural styles available for dealing with changing expectations and values of both the active and passive members of society. It is not only the values held and behavior expressed, but it is the culturally-guided dialectic occurring *among* changes in values and behavior as they are occurring that influences change in social process and, thereby, complicates the task of managing change. To the extent that technology facilitates or inhibits changes in values and behavior, it affects the *patterns* of values and behavior and, hence, the cultural setting for further change.

Social change, and the technological change intertwined with it, is also very much a consequence of the idiosyncrasies of individuals and of history. The societal traumas or successes that individuals or events confer on society leave their traces in the patterns of expectations and the procedures for justifying and carrying them out: they modify, even as they are modified by, the culture patterns up to that time. These sudden and unexpected concatenations of men and events will become all the more likely and all the more significant in an increasingly dense, interactive, and technologically interdependent setting. Hence, I would argue that the effects of idiosyncratic circumstances will increase as the degree of modernization increases.

What we are increasingly confronted with is a turbulent social environment. Those acting through institutions or through technology cannot know with certainty beforehand what will be the most likely or significant consequences of their acts because the social environment itself produces large effects independent of or unanticipatible from the deliberate acts of man and technology that are aimed at managing that environment. Thus, the task of cultural analysis and the application of that analysis to the management of change become extremely complicated as the secondary and tertiary consequences of the interaction of behaviors and technologies become at least as important as the initial consequences of the impact of a new technology. Managing the primary effects is, in a sense, the least of the problems involved in managing social change.

We shall examine more specifically such secondary and tertiary consequences later when we shall see that the cultural circumstances that have facilitated the development of high technology, and hence modernization, in the West now appear to be the very ones that may very well undermine most, if not all, of the social edifice as it is now constructed. As we explore the culture context for technological development and social change in the United States, it is necessary to keep in mind that the present situation is in profound flux. Essentially, all the cultural "givens" that we shall examine are now being challenged as to their moral rightness, their utility, or their priority. This questioning of the legitimacy of institutions and the beliefs used to justify their actions is profound and itself appears to be a consequence of the development of a highly technologized society.

Thus, it should be understood that in the first part of what follows, I will describe some cultural circumstances that *gave* underlying support to the development of the United States along lines that produced and responded to the impact and impress of technology. Later, we will examine some of the changes in culture that seem to be occurring and those that can be anticipated in the future during the period when the modernization we are concerned with here will be unfolding.

In summary, what I have to say is inevitably conjectural in three senses. In the first place, my comments are culture-bound and, hence, of unknown generalizability especially to Asian and Pacific cultures about which, most regretably, I am profoundly ignorant. In the second place, even within a culture perspective, the interpretations of what is happening are of unknown validity. In the third place, one can say very little about the future in view of the almost certain pervasive effects of unanticipatible events. In the interests of style, I will not precede each statement with "I think" or "it seems to me and other observers," or "it appears that." But these qualifications are always there.

With these caviats in mind, let me describe the structure of this paper. First I will discuss some culture characteristics that have encouraged technological developments in the United States. Second, with these characteristics in mind, I will look at some kinds of behaviors and institutional arrangements that support, and thereby reinforce, these culture characteristics. Third, we will consider some of the consequences today for the management of change in terms of the negative and positive consequences of the persisting culture patterns. And fourth, we will focus on the consequences anticipated for tomorrow: the inevitability of social turbulence as a source of change leading to new culture forms with a different valuing of technology, and the different behaviors and institutions for facilitating these values which will result from this process.

Let us turn to beliefs and expectations regarding the directions of technology and the nature of those who direct it. Certainly, the most pervasive assumption held about the relation of technology to the rest of society was that progress, which was believed to be the desirable and attainable direction of society, is the inevitable consequence of the use of new technologies. While lip service was given to other means for advancing the society and distressed questions were raised by some, the most popular ideology

and the general expectations were that progress would come
through technology and that progress is desirable; hence,
technology is desirable. Typically, "technology" referred to
material technology first and biological technology more
recently. Traditionally, social technology—social engineering—
has not been included in this category.

Intimately related to equating progress and the common
good with technological development was a basic optimism
about the future.[3] This optimism developed from religiously-
related beliefs that we were ideologically blessed and from
a belief that our increasingly powerful technologies would
give us the capabilities for manipulating the environment,
both man and material, to the ends we choose. This
optimism about the future pervaded not only our sense of
what we could become domestically, but also what we could
accomplish internationally. Internationally, our future was
believed secured (1) through military superiority achievable
via technological superiority, and (2) through our productivity
and the marketability of our products also achieved through
our superior technology.

A further piece of the interlocking set of supporting beliefs
and expectations about technology was that there were no
limits on the degree to which men and resources could be
harnessed to, and rewarded by, the expansion of technology.
Natural resources were thought to be infinitely replaceable
or substitutable through new technologies, and human wants
were believed infinitely expandable. Hence, the capacities
of humans to consume the products of new technology were
unlimited. Related to this state of mind was a firm belief that
the only healthy economy, hence healthy society, was one
that showed continual growth in the Gross National Product.
Since progress equals expanding technology which results in
expanding productivity, then the GNP must expand too.

This capability of technology to expand to meet old
needs and to develop new ones depended in part on the
belief that men could and should be organized to achieve

anything via technology that seemed important to achieve. The expectation was that by rationalizing activities through efficient management, accounting, and work techniques and, more recently, through operations research, systems analysis, computers, and the like, men could be organized to carry out enormously complex activities that would result in the development and application of new technologies. The invention of arranging men into inventing organizations was, for the most part, a World War II development, and belief in the prowess of this organizational technology to develop other technologies has grown rapidly since then and will continue to grow in most corporate and government quarters. The most recent expression of this expectation is the often-repeated assertion that putting a man on the moon demonstrates that we really can accomplish what we want, if we only have the will to do so. This view, which makes social reality just another version of technological reality, is so obviously distorted that its appeal can only be explained as the consequence of the kind of selective filters culture puts between men and their environment.

Since most technological development was done, or was believed to be done, through private corporations, this arrangement supported the traditional belief that a pragmatic, entrepreneurial, free-enterprise approach was a more reliable and rewarding path to progress than was government planning. The evidence was ample that men and machines could be organized opportunistically to produce other machines to deal with new problems and opportunities. Since American success with the development and use of technology had been experienced chiefly through the entrepreneurial, pragmatic set of beliefs and behaviors about how to do things, there was little incentive for, and deep cultural resistances against, shifting to a government planning approach for choosing among technologies to be exploited in the public interest. The way to progress was through the ad hoc interaction of private interests, each exploiting technological possibilities as the opportunities appeared attractive to them.

Now let us look at some behaviors in their individual and institutionalized forms which expressed and supported these patterned expectations and values regarding technology and which made them into self-fulfilling prophecies. Characteristic of the arrangements defining a culture, these discouraged examination and implementation of alternative societal arrangements.

Perhaps the most crucial factor was the institutionalization of the Protestant ethic, which, according to at least one influential and seminal interpretation of the history of the West, encouraged compulsive attention to entrepreneurial activities, since the evidence of eventual access to a heavenly after-life was demonstrated through success in this world.[4] Entrepreneurial motivations and opportunities were furthered by the expanding variety of possibilities for success that technology made possible. In a nontechnological society, the means for demonstrating accomplishment were prescribed and limited. In a society exploiting technology, the opportunities were unlimitedly great for developing new markets and discovering new uses for the capabilities of the technologies, and they were so used. In this way, the exploitation of technology required the development of complementary new life styles, roles, and statuses.

Facilitating this was the high value placed by the culture on achieving status rather than being legitimized by an ascribed status.[5] Evidences that people were valued for their personal achievements, rather than for their family or clan affiliations, contributed to the belief, at least among white people, that one *could* achieve success and to fulfillment of that belief. Since there were comparatively few barriers of tradition and privilege which obstructed the achievement of success through one's abilities to manipulate the natural and social environment, and since many ways of manipulating the environment were new, made possible by the technology, more opportunities for achievement were always arising. These new ways would have been inhibited if tradition, convention, and status by ascription had dominated the value system.

Mass public education was a third institutional form for producing behavior that furthered the beliefs and expectations about the utility and consequences of using technology. Mass education ingrained expectations and behavior for roles as producers and as consumers. Thereby, many people learned skills that could be applied to production, to the management of production via new technologies, and to the creation of new technologies. Equally important, they learned a set of values that stressed the desirability of consuming the products of the technologies, and the capabilities of technology to provide the basis for an ever-increasing standard of living, national prowess, and Gross National Product. Fundamentally, American mass education was designed to incorporate immigrants into the dominant culture style and, thereby, to produce people in resonance with the technological and managerial requirements of the times.

In recent years, the invention of management technologies designated to forward technological development more efficiently has reinforced the beliefs about technology, national growth, and its management. Management-facilitating systems are developed and disseminated by business schools, organizations providing current information about new management techniques, private organizations that train executives in specific management techniques, and many periodicals. More recently, the management field has included techniques such as program budgeting and planning, operations research, and systems analysis. Some of these techniques first demonstrated their utility during World War II and subsequently in the U.S. Department of Defense. Again, the high status accorded to technology applied to national

security has served to give initial legitimacy to these techniques, i.e., if they are good for defense technology they must also be good for other parts of society.

Related to this set of managerial behavior technologies is the style of behavior deemed appropriate for members of task-oriented groups or corporate entities. Largely culturally determined, this style puts heavy emphasis on rational behavior and the repression of the emotions. This emphasis on the rational with its concomitant repudiation of feelings in interpersonal relations has been demonstrated to be very costly to effective management.[6] Nevertheless, so strong has been the cultural cannon against showing feelings in task-oriented, interpersonal behavior that only recently have some organizations begun to experiment with more creative forms of management. There is a small but growing application of knowledge about group process and interpersonal behavior to the technology of managing technology, and, there are many experiments under way with new management forms and new ways of operating task groups at all levels of organization.

While these techniques appear to have demonstrated considerable ability to increase organizational efficiency and flexibility, they carry with them two important consequences. On the one hand, there is the tendency for these techniques to be used to manipulate people into more efficient "cogs" in the organization; that is, organization-development technology is used with the intent of altering people in the same spirit as technology is used to alter inanimate forms of matter. Necessarily, this corrodes those values in the American culture that emphasize the integrity and autonomy of the individual. On the other hand, since these techniques also tend to facilitate more widespread participation in decision-making they tend to lead to revisions in the definitions of power and status and the arrangements that support and enforce them. It is not mere coincidence that efforts at participant management, sensitivity training, T-group training, and so on shade-off into encounter groups and a variety of experimental activities that attract people seeking new ways of life that often reject the technological and the bureaucratic.

An important consequence of the circumstances we have been discussing has been that most people in the United States have experienced the consequences of technological development chiefly through personal purchases of items that enhance their sense of well-being. Since technology enhances their sense of well-being, they tend to project their personal experiences onto the whole society. That is, they feel a rewarding relationship with technology since they are able to select from an increasing number of rewarding options as a result of a higher standard of living in large part created by greater productivity resulting from better technologies. Thus, individuals who can afford the personal benefits of technology have been drawn away, so to speak, from attending to the appalling consequences the accumulation of affluent, individual choices have had on the natural and human environment as a whole. This selective perception contributes to the lack of institutional arrangements for the support of technologies for the public welfare which cannot depend for direct support on the existence of a market clientele. This is most evident in the areas of pollution control and environmental quality in general as well as in areas such as mass transport, low-cost housing, and truly good education. There are, of course, other obstructions to the development of public welfare technologies. Some arise from corporate preoccupation with products that involve minimum risk and reorganization; in government agencies they amount to analogous preoccupations with bureaucratic protection of their special constituencies. But, overall, the emphasis on private consumption and the rewards of private consumption, which encourage that emphasis, have discouraged attention to investment in social welfare technology.

These expectancies and values about technology, interacting with technological developments and other processes in the society, evolved into the form we recognize today of a highly developed technological society with enormous, indeed, outrageous disparities between its greatest and its least accomplishments. These disparities offer increasing evidence of the inadequacy of just these life styles we have reviewed for trying to manage social change partially through the use of technology. What is becoming clear to observers, including some in government and industry, is the absolute need for some sort of *planned* social change, for long-range planning that extends over a decade or more. But this need implies an equally pressing need for basic changes in the values and expectations held and behaviors practiced—the culture pattern—so that social change management philosophies and activities can be implemented in a very short time. The short time requirement seems crucial: as I shall argue subsequently, it appears that, in the United States, survival of a social system based on our conventional interpretation of a democratic philosophy is highly problematic, and the risks to its survival are becoming greater the longer it takes to get major changes implemented in the management of that society. Note that I am not saying that the technology for social, long-range planning presently exists. Rather, I am saying that the *beginnings* of such a technology do exist and the necessary circumstances for its further development depend on deliberate efforts to utilize and refine it. To date, these efforts have been lacking for the most part.

The development of the United States under a culture pattern that encouraged an essentially ad hoc, laissez-faire approach to technological elaboration, appears to have produced a state of affairs of such complexity and difficulty that it is really impossible to see how to get from the present into a desirable future in a coherent, deliberate, and politically democratic manner. In effect, the United States faces enormous problems pertinent to the management of change, problems of modernization or, better, post-modernization, that are analogous to those in Asia and the Pacific. It is increasingly evident that, just as many culture values in other parts of the world are contradictory to the conditions needed for modernization, so too the traditional culture pattern in the United States is contradictory to the conditions necessary for postmodernization. Our crises in governance, in the management of control and freedom, are similar to those in other parts of the world that are far less dependent on high technology.

Let us, therefore, now attend to those residual traditional values and styles which seem contradictory to the needs of today, to the needs of a society in important part created out of the interactions of those traditional values and styles.

First, there is widespread resistance to long-range planning by government. Planning as perceived within the traditional set of behaviors and values implies control, loss of autonomy, and loss of those entrepreneurial conditions which have allowed so many people to become so successful, often at the expense of so many others, and to jeopardize the natural environment to which man's survival is ultimately linked. The resistance to planning grows out of the state of mind associated with the learned success of non-planned approaches to societal development, and out of an apprehensiveness toward risking restrictions on "doing one's own thing," to use the contemporary phrase. The resistance to planning also derives from the positive value put on one meaning of pragmatism. For Americans, pragmatism is often perceived as the equivalent of expedient activity sufficient to the moment at hand. It is much less often perceived as the proper philosophy for evaluating in a longer time context the appropriateness of the means used. Many people raised and rewarded by the traditional culture view their world as one that is still relatively segregated and relatively non-interdependent; they expect that there always will be room for expansion (the frontier philosophy), that social interdependence is low, that what there is is encompassible (the small town, low population, and low event-density philosophy), and that whatever goes wrong can be rectified by further deliberate actions (the optimistic, "technological-fix" philosophy). All of these expectations and reinforcing behaviors sustain a lack of appreciation for the need for interactive, interdependent behavior, and hence for planned behavior. Planned behavior is needed to compensate for the absence of culturally defined behavior and values that, of themselves, would constrain behavior to that which is compatible with high levels of interdependence and interaction. Such a culture pattern does not exist for most of the population.

In the light of what we know about how attitudes and beliefs are reinforced, such values will follow *after* experiences which make one kind of living rewarding and another punishing. Probably, we shall have to plan first and then, out of the consequent experiences in living with these plans, may grow the values that can replace part of the planning behavior itself. If people learn to live in ways that assume intense interdependency, then behaviors that are expected and valued will of themselves serve some of the directing purposes that planning now would substitute for.

Another increasingly inappropriate culture style still offers substantial rewards for most of those who have grown up within it: this is the hierarchical structure which characterizes interpersonal and intraorganizational relationships in most organizations, in particular in corporations and government. The essentially pyramidal organizational arrangement grew out of more primitive culture patterns of family structure and predatory and defense tactics. It was reasonably applicable to comparatively simple organizations with stable task allocations and simple response patterns, a situation that also characterized the earlier years of technology utilization. Furthermore, the bureaucratic structures associated with organizational pyramids did have the virtue of rationalizing the services the organization provided by insulating the organization from the environment. It insulated the organization, in part, in order to limit the amount of disruptive information coming into the organization so that there would be sufficient organizational stability to respond to stable environmental demands. This, thereby, made services, particularly those provided by governments, less subject to corruption and caprice, and more reliable. However, as a result of the development of an increasingly differentiated environment that made an increasing variety of demands on the institutions serving it, and as a result of the increasing number of consequences produced when these institutions insert new technologies into the society without sufficient preplanning and control, the bureaucratic structure has become, by its very nature, comparatively rigid and unresponsive.

What are now needed are "disruptable" organizations, so to speak, which are better able to respond to a variety of rapidly changing demands from the environment by being better able to make transformations within the organization. The pyramidal structure, the bureaucratic structure, cannot accomplish this. But, it is particularly difficult to shift structures when organizations feel themselves challenged, besieged, under stress—the conditions of today. When confronted with such challenges, those who have succeeded by leading organizations to their present condition usually try to retreat, in a typical human manner, to patterns of behavior which worked in the past. For that very reason, they are unlikely to work in the present. But short of catastrophe and deep crises, when organizations seem most open to change, the tendency is to cling to rigid, unresponding structures.

Closely related to the conditions just described is the set of values and expectancies in the culture that traditionally has made it difficult, if not impossible, for public and political figures to acknowledge, to embrace, error in public. That is, United States tradition sets a high value on not being wrong and, indeed, partly defines its leaders as those who have the ability to be right. Error has an aura of sinfullness about it or, at least, of reprehensible inadequacy. Hence, public figures pretend error didn't happen or, if it did, it was someone else's fault. Error is punished; success is rewarded. The belief that one *ought* to be able to succeed is especially reinforced by expectations about our ability to control our actions, expectations applied to the human realm that derive from successes we have come to expect in the technological realm. Many counterproductive consequences thereby arise. In particular, there is great reluctance throughout government and corporations to be truly innovative because the uncertainty in the situation is so high that the chance of error is also high. Thus, it is seldom worth the personal or economic risk for successful members of organizations to champion innovation when circumstances are sufficiently rewarding without doing so.

Embracing error as a positive virtue is a requirement for effective long-range social planning because all such planning, if it is to be humane and responsive to reality, must be flexible with regard to revaluation of goals and priorities and the means for realizing them. Planning must include an explicit moral obligation to learn from what goes wrong. Such an approach, which assumes that the future is highly uncertain, runs contrary to the deep-lying optimism referred to earlier. It also runs contrary to the pragmatic definition that one can always rectify a situation and that "too little and too late" is not really a plausible outcome.

One basic cultural shift required to make error-embracing feasible would place social experiment and social development ahead of re-election. Politicians at all levels in the United States set—and traditionally are expected to set—re-election as their prime obligation and have seldom been known to jeopardize re-election in the interest of more tenuous, long-range aims for this society. Clearly, such a shift in political values and styles would necessitate profound changes in the

American social system. Among other things, it would carry with it the need for long-range political stability in order to cope with short-range, as well as long-range, social turbulence. How these needs might be reconciled is completely unknown at this time.

In addition to the counterproductive residual cultural characteristics, there are residual cultural characteristics which are especially compatible with the requirements for the management of social change in a postmodernized society. In the first place, traditional modes of optimism and pragmatism can operate as culture characteristics that *encourage* shifts in values towards planning and the gathering of social information as a basis for taking action. That is, some spokesmen take the position that there are great things that we should and can do and that these will take longer to do and are more important to do than other things we have done. They feel that we have to get organized to do them; that we must plan so we can do them. So far, this mood is chiefly rhetoric and it remains to be seen whether those espousing this value position will be able to recruit and develop the behavior needed in others or, indeed, if they themselves understand the implications of their position. However, one indication that this movement may gain strength is the increasing attention being given to the need to collect social indicator data as a basis for knowing what is happening and for doing something about it. Since such data reflect both the moment and change over time, they are necessary (but not sufficient) for planning. Also encouraging are expressions in Congress and professional organizations of the need for, and interest in, doing longer-range technological assessments as a basis for deciding whether or not it is in the societal interest to produce particular technologies and how to apply them. This, too, is still at the rhetorical or at the introductory legislative stage and it remains to be seen how seriously these new value priorities will be taken when the changes in behavior needed to fulfill them become explicit.

The value placed on achieved status over ascribed status can be seen as carrying with it an inherent questioning of legitimacy whenever any of those who have achieved status are encouraged to retain it so long and so unquestioningly that it becomes, in effect, ascribed at least to the extent that the behaviors and values associated with it are treated as if they were self-evident and unquestionable. Hence, the questioning of legitimacy which is presently disrupting the United States also carries with it the potential for reallocation of status and power and the values that underly these, and, thereby, the potential for organizational invention and innovation. The potential for social experimentation is great within this mood of questioning legitimacy. But so too is the potential for social disaster through the disolution of existing shared patterns of expected behavior. Without such shared patterns men are unable to assign priorities and allocate resources over long enough time periods and on a large enough scale to meet social needs even poorly.

As suggested earlier, the development of a management technology bodes both well and ill. It is worth discussing again in this context as an example of a favorable expression of a residual traditional culture pattern when related to the pragmatic approach and to the belief in the virtues of technology. In the management technology field there are a number of humanitarian psychologists and executives eager to enhance the opportunities in job settings for creativeness and fulfilling work. As a result, a number of experiments are under way which attempt to redefine conventional organizational power to allow participants the scope to be more productive and creative. These experiments depend on the deliberate, self-conscious examination of self working with others, task-group processes, and shared goal-setting responsibilities. As such, these efforts are in the rational tradition of the West, in the technological, optimistic tradition which treats self as something capable of deliberate change and growth. This need not necessarily demean the sense of individuality. Indeed, it is an opportunity to enhance sense of self and of others since an atmosphere of trust is produced and, with it, greater incentives to risk uncertainty and innovation. These experiments in both voluntaristic and corporate settings appear to be rewarding in terms of personal satisfactions and organizational effectiveness.

I will turn now to anticipating some consequences of the interplay between the positive and negative aspects of these residual culture values as they may affect the place of technology and the management of social change. In this way, we will see additional challenges that a postmodernized society faces in dealing with the culture premises which have made it a highly technologized society. And, since one way or another the modernizing nations will have to deal with whatever conditions exist in the postmodernized societies, we will better appreciate also the additional challenges for those nations seeking to modernize themselves. It is in this way that futurist conjectures become essentially pertinent for modernizing efforts. For, while it can be argued that the most pressing problems of these nations are those that exist right now, these problems, by their very nature, will only be solved in the future—five, ten, twenty years from now. They exist now, but they cannot be solved now. Hence, plausible future circumstances become crucial for planning now how to resolve these problems over future years. Plausible future circumstances become the context for choosing among alternative procedures for planning solutions to present problems. Thus, the future is the present for modernizers. It can only be ignored if the future is assumed to be the same as the present. And, as we shall see, the future of the postmodernized societies is certain to be much different from the present and past situation. Thereby, the situation will also be different for modernizing societies to the extent they will be interdependent with the postmodernized societies.

All evidence suggests that, at least for the next couple of decades, the United States will be a highly turbulent society more likely than not, demoralizing itself into a splintered, culturally amorphous state of chronic social crises and catastrophe. The turmoil arises from an increasing questioning of the premises underlying the society and from the divergent and various behaviors associated with that questioning. At the same time, there is a growing lack of adequate forms of governance, negotiation, mediation, and constructive control. This lack can be ascribed to three general conditions.

First, the very challenging of the premises of the culture from so many and from such widely diverse sources as young versus old, black versus white, rich versus poor, and white collar versus blue collar, presents the society with a situation that a viable culture patterning does not face, by and large—namely, its own undermining. Hence, there are no institutions that are really effective for dealing with this state of affairs. Dissent has always been constrained to expression and action within the rules of the game. Now dissent includes rejection of the rules. The culture has no means for coping adequately with its own rejection, so to speak.

Second, we are subject to a new property in this type of social system: because of large population size and the high frequency of repetitive events, very small percents of people or events now become socially perturbing. This is so whether it be an unlikely but now frequent tanker break-up or ghetto riots or protests by a small percent of housewives, hard hats, or hippies.

Third, there is the very complexity and interdependence, the fragility of the society, with its vulnerability to the unanticipated adverse consequences of technologies whether it be oil leaks, inversion layers, nuclear explosions, or the high-speed exchange of emotions, made possible by TV. There are no adequate forms of governance for comprehending, anticipating, and dealing with the scale, variety, and speed of interactiveness of the men and events in the society. Hence, all traditional approaches are likely to be relatively inadequate, and all new approaches are likely to have a high rate of failures as would any experiments performed under such relatively blind and complicated conditions. Thus, United States society is bound to be in a state of continual high turmoil.

Add to this the longer-range unanticipated ecological burdens imposed on the environment and the men in it by the sheer numbers of people using, wasting, and polluting their environment. Add further the more obvious consequences of thermal pollution from nuclear reactors and other forms of environmental distortion from chemical pollutants. Necessarily, either the environment will steadily deteriorate, thereby multiplying the turbulence of the social situation, or a major reallocation of resources will have to be put into preserving the environment. Such a reallocation will impose novel behavioral constraints on large numbers of organizations, people, and styles of life. This will further increase turbulences.

In such a societal and environmental situation we can expect alternative and simultaneous periods of repression and license as the society, through formal and informal modes of governance, tries to cope with turbulence either by repressing it or allowing freer reign. The former approach cannot solve the problem of turbulence: repression will generate reactive turbulence since the society is too big and too heterogeneous to repress totally. License generates social frictions, unpredictability, and, thereby, more turbulence. But it also provides opportunities for discovering and synthesizing new styles of conduct. There is, to my mind, a slight hope—but only a slight hope—that from these, with luck and wisdom and deliberate research, we will learn enough about the appropriate culture base for such a society to be able to establish the conditions for managing a society of this complexity. What that set of values and expectancies might be is not presently evident. There may be glimmers of its characteristics in the behavior of some of the groups of young people with their experiments in sharing and commune life. However, these expressions seem to be more residues of past Utopian ideals, derived from a simpler day when the facts of technology and social complexity did not exist.

If a stable culture pattern is developed, it is entirely reasonable to expect that technology will no longer be seen as an inherently positive expression of man which should be left to its own efflorescence and proliferation. Rather, technology and its development and utilization will be increasingly a matter subject to careful evaluation in a setting of human need values that are more primary and determining. To ask what these values and procedures would be and when they will be in operation would be much like asking members of feudal culture to characterize the yet-to-be-evolved culture based on a money and market economy. They simply couldn't do so: the experiences upon which to base the concepts didn't exist.

As the United States and, quite possibly, Europe and other highly industrialized areas go through the anguish and crises of discovering that their culture bases are inadequate for providing the rewards, goals, and governance needed in a highly technologized society, these traditional Western culture models will become increasingly less attractive to those areas of Asia and the Pacific seeking to modernize themselves. The cost of technological modernization, United States style, will become more evident to them as time goes on. But, the costs of not modernizing are already evident. Confronted with this dilemma, we can expect that all areas of the world will have to struggle with the terrible and exciting challenge of trying to discover forms of life and the values underlying them that one can reasonably hope will provide the rewards of technologically based society without the outrageous costs which are becoming more and more evident. The outcome of that struggle is, to my mind, unpredictable. If it is successful, the culture forms will very likely be quite different from what we might imagine them to be.

The task will be extraordinarily difficult—if it can be done deliberately at all. Whatever else it requires, it is necessary that men in power come to use knowledge about society's workings, about future possibilities, about themselves, far more broadly and easily than now is the case.[7] Contrary to the myth in the West that "if you build a better mouse trap, the world will beat a path to your door," the clear facts are that the inventor usually has to drag the world kicking and screaming to even look at his trap. This is especially true when we are talking about getting knowledge used that is innovative with regard to man and society: cultures are designed to screen out all but certain innovations, as the earlier quotations from Kluckhohn emphasize. So far, it looks like both Eastern and Western cultures are designed to screen out innovations of the sort that would be needed to manage humanely a huge world of men and machines, but of limited resources.

If we are to find a way out, it will require that we come to value highly the application of new knowledge about men and institutions. We are developing some technology that facilitates knowledge utilization but for the most part we simply know better than we did how little we know about such a technology. This technology needs to be applied to changing institutions and organizations so that they can effectively meet the changed conditions that render them inadequate, so that they can do long-range planning, and so that they—the men in them—can easily embrace error and quickly learn therefrom. We now have the beginnings of a technology for changing organizations—but only a beginning. And we need to develop a technology for designing institutions and organizations that can respond effectively and humanely to the turbulent environment I described earlier. With regard to this requirement, we do not have even the beginnings of such a technology: We are only beginning to develop the theory.[8]

I can only conclude that, given our problems in the East and West, and given our primitive social technologies for dealing with them, we are bound to experience more social turbulence and many social calamities. This social context means that it will be harder to do the research and development needed to improve the social technologies described above. However, disasters and crises provide the easiest occasion to initiate organizational innovations and value changes. The problem is to be ready beforehand with the means for increasing the likelihood of establishing the desired change when the disaster provides the opportunity. But this means putting a major effort into crises and postdisaster planning. And this requires acknowledging that the chances are poor of averting crises and disaster, and that we must prepare for the worst. Men in positions of leadership and power have an almost impossible time doing this. In terms of the culture values East and West, such acknowledgment is politically suicidal. At a deeper level, such acknowledgment means that successful men — including you and me — must accept that their very image of themselves as successful is now and henceforth wrong. We must acknowledge that we really know very little about how to deal creatively with tomorrow. We need to acknowledge that, somehow, we have discovered and are ensnared in a new wilderness, a new jungle, and that the skills that got us here are inadequate to get us out. Looking around us, we must acknowledge that we really are lost.

Will we find our way out? That depends at least on recognizing that we do not know where we are, and on drastically reordering our beliefs and behaviors so that we can begin to try to find out. This reorganization itself may not be enough; it may not come in time. But it is the least we can do and the first thing we must do. Can we do it? I doubt it, but none of us understands the dynamics of societies well enough to be sure. So I shall continue to try.

Notes and References

1   Clyde Kluckhohn and William H. Kelly, The concept of culture, in *The Science of Man in the World Crisis,* Columbia Univ. Press, New York (1945), pp. 78-106.

2   It should be kept in mind that in all but the simplest cultures there are subcultures. These share the major patterns of the culture they are part of, but they also possess different characteristics than do other subcultures within the culture. The relationships among the subcultures are patterned and the distinctive characteristics of the subcultures serve specific functions within the overall culture pattern. For example, in complex societies the culture characteristics of the intellectuals differ from, say, those of rural people, but, within a society, they share certain beliefs and behaviors and their interrelationships are patterned.

3   Robert L. Heilbroner, Optimism and the idea of the future, in *The Future as History,* Grove Press, New York (1961), pp. 16-18.

4   R. H. Tawney, *Religion and the Rise of Capitalism,* Harcourt Brace, New York (1926); since reprinted in several paperback editions.

5   Talcott Parsons, An analytical approach to the theory of social stratification, in *Essays in Sociological Theory Pure and Applied,* Free Press, Glencoe, ill. (1949), pp. 166-184.

6   Chris Argyris, *Organization and Innovation,* Dorsey Press, Homewood, ill. (1965).

7   I am referring specifically to scientific knowledge. But I am also including that knowledge that has to do with values and, thereby, with alternative definitions of the nature of man and the worthy life.

8   The general problem of redesigning organizations so that they can learn to do long-range social planning is examined in detail in D. Michael, *On Learning to Plan-and Planning to Learn: The Social Psychology of Changing Toward Future Responsive Societal Learning,* Jossey-Bass, San Francisco (1973).

Forecasting and Planning in an Incoherent Context

Introduction

incoherent: lack of coherence; lacking cohesion; not sticking together; not logically integrated, consistent, and intelligible; disjointed; rambling; incongruous.
Webster's New World Dictionary, College Edition

CERTAINLY our society and plausibly our civilization can be characterized as being increasingly incoherent. Its aspirations and activities do not integrate with one another, do not cohere conceptually, operationally, linguistically, or psychodynamically. The contributing circumstances described here will continue to exacerbate the situation—themselves being disjointed, rambling, vis-a-vis each other, even though they share some characteristics that also contribute to the dislocations.

In this light consider the chief function of forecasts and planning: to enhance focus, direction—coherence—for whatever ends. To accomplish this function requires a material and symbolic context that can be rendered coherent. But there is no prospect of removing the incoherences for the foreseeable future, given the nature of the sources and their reinforcement by the circumstances they engender. One cannot lead unless circumstances produce those who wish to be led; so, too, with the potential usefulness of forecasts and planning. Nevertheless, the unfastened circumstances that constitute our incoherent situation will, singly and in combination, result in more need and requests for these services. But because of the incoherences, the sought-after products and processes are unlikely to be either fruitful or enduring. The pressures for short-term responses to critical issues will also increase and, given the incoherences, dominate social action. Indeed, the presence of forecasts and planning efforts will further complicate the context, if they have much effect at all.

In order to "say" about these incoherences, I conjure three categories: epistemological, social, and psychodynamic. In order that forecasts and planning have the potential for enhancing coherence, it is necessary that these categories or contexts be compatible; that each can depend on the other for illumination, confirmation, and collaboration, that they are "talking about" recognizably related matters. Alternatively, it must be possible to ignore or repress the incompatibilities between them. I shall argue that neither requirement can be met: these contexts are explicitly and mutually incoherent, and in the case of the social category, internally fragmented as well.

Epistemological Incoherence

I have explored this matter in more detail elsewhere with regard to futures studies and forecasting[1,2] and with regard to planning[3]; here I will summarize. A society's epistemology derives from and sustains its mythology, its social construction of reality[4]. Its mythology defines how the "world" works, and why it is as it is, and to what ends. The mythology that has shaped Western culture asserts that the world is controllable (including the human component) because it operates according to lawful processes, expressed as relations between cause and effect. While the prevailing myth has its detractors and would-be challengers, it still dominates; so much of what we are and do is embedded in its way of making sense of life. And it has worked very well for a portion of humankind, white males especially. In particular, we still presume, even if tacitly, a determinable, undergirding lawfulness of cause and effect in the human realm. This presumption is strong enough, at least in the minds of those who look to forecasts and attempt longer ranging planning, to shape their actions and expectations. But if human activity is describable as sequences of causes and effects in the way other processes seem to be, we are a very long way from any theory of social or individual change under turbulent conditions, as is demonstrated by our inability to forecast birth rates and by the disarray in economic theory[5,6]*. I subscribe to Polanyi's argument that creative human activities have an emergent quality: the "whole" is unpredictably "greater" than the sum of the parts[7]. This seems obvious in the conduct of art, science and politics and in interpersonal relations. One cannot predict a new theory or art form or new political and personal developments from what has gone before. Nor can one predict the consequences of predictions about the consequences[8]. After the new state of affairs has emerged, interpretations arise that purport to relate causes and effects so as to connect the new condition to what preceded it. But such interpretations do not arise before the new state of affairs emerges[9]. But even if it should prove possible to represent some aspects of aggregate human behavior through the new chaos theory, our ability to predict or control that behavior will be slight because of the very circumstances that characterize chaotic processes. Moreover, humans experiencing chaotic processes through the peephole of their consciousness and the depths of their unconsciousness cannot act toward those chaotic circumstances as they would if they were merely observing them from outside. They/we live in them and are not about to wait out the painful and problematic transformations.

---

*   For example, much of our description and theory about human behavior, and thereby our forecasts and planning and policy, depend upon, and are justified by, findings from interview surveys. Yet, it has been shown recently that neither open-ended interviews (where the respondents rank their responses to categories that they differentiate) nor closed-ended interviews (where the respondent ranks categories specified by the interviewer) produce data that can be used to infer "either absolute levels or even relative orderings of public choices" (i.e., priorities, preferences, concerns, etc.) with regard to the categories queried about[31].

The epistemological crises run deeper still. The ideas and evidence from the de-constructionists in literary theory[10], the constructionists in social psychology[11], and the cognitive linguists[12] argue that any edifice of ideas constructed and expressed in words is ungrounded in "objective reality." It is grounded only in communal agreement on other categories and words; indeed the very category of "objective reality" is but a verbal construct, a metaphor generated from other metaphors and leading only to other metaphors[13]. It seems that, no matter how we try to do otherwise, when we write or talk, we are writing or talking about words which, in turn, are anchored only in other words rather than in "objective reality." Not only is the map not the territory, but "map" and "territory" are not "real" either.

> "Knowledge can now be seen as something that the organism builds up in the attempt to order the as such amorphous flow of experience by establishing repeatable experiences and relatively stable relations between them. The possibilities of constructing such an order are determined and perpetually constrained by the preceding steps in the construction. This means that the 'real' world manifests itself exclusively there where our constructions break down. But since we can describe and explain these breakdowns only in the very concepts we have used to build the failing structures, this process can never yield a picture of a world which we could hold responsible for their failure."[14]

What is important here is not only these ideas per se but also that recognition of them and appreciation of their enormous implications for the legitimacy of the processes of governance will spread to a widening audience of thinkers, the very people who brood about the utility and validity and hence the ethics of forecasting and planning[15]. If sophisticated thinking is to continue to have a place in social policy formulation, strategic planning and evaluation, then sooner or later these ideas are going to begin to challenge the whole process and purpose of these activities. The clash between traditional thinking about social reality and

the meaning of words and the new thinking about these
matters will further compound the incoherences. (Here,
I acknowledge again that my words are not exempt. Nor
are those of any other "sayer." Such is the nature of the
incoherences confronting us: if we take seriously the words
of those who are saying about the nature of saying, the more
we say, the more questionable becomes what we say. If I
haven't misinterpreted him, Churchman[16] anticipated this
years ago when he argued that it was reason that was the
great challenge to reason.)

Some Sources of Social Incoherence

THE story of the eroding but still dominant myth that
undergirds our social construction of reality and its
associated epistemological footlessness can be told as a
conjuration of growing social discontinuities. These do not
point in any one direction; they contradict, conflict with and
slew past each other, and they amplify each other. They call
for, encourage, obstruct, and undermine the feasibility of
forecasting and planning.

Ozone depletion, greenhouse effects, terrorism,
fresh water shortages, mal-education, substance abuse,
AIDS, joint-regulation of urban transportation and urban
growth, crime, the multiple consequences of diverging age
distributions, and an absence of third world employment
opportunities are some examples of a multiplying
collection of circumstances, all of which require enormous
expenditures of thought, effort, and money to even begin
to ameliorate. What is clear is that, within our prevailing
perspective, all entail vastly expanded material and
operational infrastructures for coordination, regulation,
collaboration and social invention. The longer remedial
actions are delayed, the more costly the solutions, if indeed
there are such, the farther off in the future the rewards
for current sacrifices, and the more interconnected the

outcomes. Since the gains and losses deriving therefrom have chiefly to do with the creation, distribution and protection of public goods, the political risks will be very great especially since the outcome of any major effort will be problematic, subject to unknown systemic and chaotic processes and idiosyncratic events.

Yet, we lack concepts of governance, political incentives and a system of values for undertaking much more than a bits-and-pieces approach[17,18].

> " 'The human mind,' Jay Forrester says, 'is unable to understand human social systems.' This is true. Our innate conceptions were selected to cope with the modest causal environment of our animal ancestors. But they are inadequate for dealing with the responsibilities our current technocracy presumes in this world. Our one-dimensional causal thinking is unqualified to find a solution. Society therefore constructs social truths and causes that alternatively cancel each other out, and the decision is still in the hands of that blind power which, let us admit it, fills us all with fear."[19]

Not only do we lack concepts of governance appropriate for guiding an increasingly interconnected world, but more to the point, we lack concepts appropriate for governance during the period of incoherence, with its attendant turbulence and disruption, during the transition from now to whatever and whenever more coherent forms might emerge. Nevertheless, this turbulent period is precisely when, in the disjointed and ad hoc ways characteristic of this society, various organizations will turn to help from forecasts and planning (or to that form of forecasting and planning called "crisis management") in the hope that somehow, with such help, they will regain control of what they misperceive as *their* environment of rights and opportunities. Unraveling these efforts, of course, will be the familiar political pressures that result in too many incoherent attempts at quick fixes.

Running counter to the requirements for coordination and collaboration will continue to be the demands at all levels—from the person to the nation-state—for autonomy, sovereignty, decentralization, competitive edge, rights, liberation, and freedom-from and freedom-to. These aspirations and demands are, of course, encouraged and legitimated by belief in, or recourse to, those attributes of the still dominant Western myth that separate cause and effect, subject and object, we and they, and which make the world out to be either/or rather than both/and when it comes to values and beliefs. As participants in this social construction of reality, these demands are reinforced and endorsed by the media's adversarial approach to news, as well as by the norms of the judicial/legal system.

No doubt proponents of many causes or groups will seek help via forecasts and planning to further their own ends. But if the creators of such services have the intelligence and integrity to recognize the limitations as well as the value of such separatist intentions in an increasingly interdependent world, the client is not likely to be very pleased with the confrontations to concept and purpose such services should provide.

An increasingly interconnected world—and whether or not this is a useful way to perceive it, we are stuck with that perception, given our epistemology and language structure— will require resetting system and subsystem boundaries to whatever is appropriate for the welfare, and the coherence, of the emerging interdependencies. But resetting boundaries means shifts in the allocation of power and status, shifts sure to be resisted and challenged, adding to the turmoil and the incoherence.

Underlying these difficulties is the deeper incoherence— what values should determine the appropriate location of system boundaries? Currently there is no coherent set of shared values within the Western world, much less worldwide. In particular there is no operating system of shared values that presumes a both/and, interactive, interdependent human condition. Instead, survival of the fittest contends with being thy sibling's keeper. As MacIntyre[20] has demonstrated, all we possess are remnants of previously demolished value systems. Nothing holds these remnants together so we are left with personal preferences applied to inconsistent collections of irreconcilable bits and pieces from the past. While ecological and psychodynamic understanding[21,22] point in constructive directions, there is nothing remotely available on which to base a value system that must adjudicate among and reconcile a human environment that is partly chaotic, partly systemic, and partly punctuated in its processes and purposes and mostly unconscious in its motivations and reactions[23].

This is no mere moralist's headache. It is the values held by a person, organization and society that determine what information is important, what interpretations are useful, and what actions acceptable. Indeed, values determine what defines a "problem" or "opportunity" or "challenge" and the ways of responding to them. They are a fundamental way in which the social construction of reality is operationalized and reinforced. Even when not explicit or acknowledged, they select perspectives and proposals, and as Vickers showed[24], the facts bolstering both. (I trust it is evident that legal decisions or legislation do not obviate the question of what values should prevail. Abiding by judicial decisions or specific laws are themselves value-based choices often in contention. And precedent and legal constructions of reality are having a demonstrably difficult time authoritatively dealing with the issues arising out of the incoherences described here.)

Consider, too, that more complexity plus more (inevitably) incomplete information about the human condition encourages selecting from these multiple, confusing and uncertain signals those most compatible with one's preferred ways of perceiving and evaluating the world. The number of blind persons and the number of elephants subject to interpretation increase; grounds for choice and action multiply, legitimated by whatever values from our splintered collection that are forwarded as "reasonable" and "rational." Conventional technical/logical rationality or, as Linstone[25] labels it, the "technical perspective" is only one value priority. Alternative rationalities also claiming priority prevail as well, such as protecting organizational turf, political expediency, employment protection, or power acquisition. Other examples include the familiar safety of habit, or religious belief, or ideological commitment, or culturally given norms of "acceptability." All such value priorities shift and cut across organizations and individuals and, most assuredly, those persons who play leadership roles.

Living with the incoherences constructively and humanely and attempting to transcend them will require extraordinarily mature leaders/guides and followers/citizens. However, many parents at all socioeconomic levels—it is not only a matter of economic deprivation—contribute to the incoherence. They make poor or negative contributions to the shaping of a next generation able to grow into emotionally mature, cognitively competent, and socially responsible adults, essential for maintaining a complex and humane world[26]. Parents do poorly because they lack the requisite values, attitudes and skills. Instead they pass on to the next generation the consequences of their own neuroses and counter-productive values and life styles.

For the most part, schools also make their contribution to incoherence. They do not educate for a citizenry competent to live with and seek ways through these incoherences. Those who act to affect the conduct of society, either through the ballot or in the streets, are mostly unable and unwilling to think with the subtlety, skill, and persistence required for critical rather than ritual participation in the conduct of governance that seeks to overcome the conditions described here[27]. At least what is required is the ability to read, write, and discourse easily and naturally, in terms of dialectical processes, systems behavior, both/and as well as either/or logics, and circular rather than linear cause-effect relationships. What is also required is at least an understanding and feeling for the basics of psychodynamics as they affect one's own behavior and that of others in the public arena. But, of course, no such educational goals or child-raising norms exist in society at large, if for no other reason than the traditional myths that guide Western societies (and most others) do not require such competencies of their members. They really have not been necessary until recent times.

In this light, in the years ahead, the conduct of governance will be increasingly bedeviled at all levels by a growing gap between what is needed and the available emotional and cognitive capabilities of leaders and led.† (That one of the functions of groups, organizations, staffs, etc. is to

---

†   This is not to say that some conventional indicators of "success" will not continue to have their ups and downs. GNP will grow, technology will create new products, more people will get university degrees, gourmet food and quality television will continue to entice their consumers, and specialized markets for egregious consumptions proliferate. But the fundamental incoherences will persist and grow under and between these categories of success.
New York City is an appropriate symptom of the accumulating disjointedness. Consider Trump Tower and homeless people, mindless consumption of glitter and hunger, a grossly deteriorating infrastructure and ever more high-rise construction, magnificent museums and problematic garbage disposal, exclusive private schools and more than 40% truancy from public high schools, endemic crime and resounding pronouncements on ethics in the New York Times, etc. Consider, too, that there is no political will to do much about it. The predicaments collide, pile up and gridlock in ever more complex disarray—the ever mounting human and dollar costs required to begin to confront them pushed out of mind, out of action, and out of meaning[32].

counteract or compensate for individual incompetencies should be of little comfort in these days of revelations of persisting misuse of personal power and the vulnerability of multi-person governance groups to the same incompetencies. After all, most of their members are the products of the traditional child-rearing and educational circumstances described here.)

Some Sources of Psychodynamic Incoherence

THOSE who live within a social construction of reality (a myth that defines the world as controllable and therefore defines the competent person as one who can control causes to produce specific effects) will go to great lengths to avoid recognizing how profoundly unconscious biological and psychological forces and cultural definitions of reality implacably shape how we think, feel and act[28]. That we are driven by unconscious, and thus uncontrolled needs, aspirations, terrors and furies has been demonstrated in many formal studies and richly explored in the West by such luminous minds as Freud, Nietzsche and Jung. (Here I am referring to unconscious, imperious, often obsessive needs such as those for power, affection, recognition, order or disorder, spiritual union, and needs to dominate or submit, to destroy or to create, to nurture or to be nurtured.) How these are expressed through individual behavior varies, of course, from socially constructive and interpersonally sensitive to pathologically evil. In part, this depends on what a given culture permits by way of "acting out" (e.g., Nero) and with what constraints or rewards the organizations within the culture surround their members (e.g., those who drive themselves to "burn out"). Today, these norms of acceptability and constraint are all in flux, a major contributor to incoherence at all levels.

Elsewhere[29] I have elaborated on the pernicious consequences of the unconscious processes of denial and projection, when these are the means by which persons who see themselves as highly competent unconsciously protect their deeply held image of themselves when faced with the enormous ambiguities, uncertainties and complexities of this world. Ideas, events or experiences that undermine that image undermine a person's very existence; it is a deep threat to one's very being. A typical way psychodynamic processes operate to cope with such a threat is by denying its existence. Denial may be accomplished by trivializing the threat so its enormity is not accepted consciously, so that the threat is not consciously noticed or acknowledged. The threat is repressed and transferred to the unconscious where it persists in disguised forms, e.g., displaced (i.e., projected) onto other less threatening "objects" such as the enemy, or taxes, or liberals or conservatives, or God's will, or the media. Thereby the person who denies is able to ignore schemes which require, in order to evaluate and act upon them, facing directly the denied threats. Moreover, by denying the overwhelming seriousness of the issues, the person who denies can reject the proposal on the grounds that it is politically infeasible or someone else's problem. Business as usual, then, is sometimes maintained by the psychodynamic processes of denial or projection.

In this way, when these processes are operative—and by no means are they always—responses in a leader or citizen mismatch the social issues or the epistemological dilemma. The response is disjointed and inappropriate in relation to the issue, and it lacks coherence across issues. Of course, this incoherence can be amplified when denial or projection make use of the already ill-fitting epistemology to justify a reaction that arises from repressed needs, fears or hopes. (If I were to give examples, such as President Reagan's obsession with SDI, or the fact that forecasts often fail to influence decision makers, the reader could claim, and might well be right, that my choice of examples and my implied criticism reflect my unconscious needs to make sense of the world in ways that result in my seeing mismatches where there are none. This is precisely the kind of incoherency we are now subject to in light of our knowledge about the stories we tell about the stories we tell!)

The main point is that forecasts or planning efforts that presume that responses to them will be, or can be, exclusively conscious and "rational" will always slew by their intended audience. They mismatch; there is a disconnect. A major consideration is left out of the dialogue: the meaning of the effort is different from what is said, or what is said about what is done, and the forecast or plan lacks congruence with the unconscious world of the recipients.

In summary, we face unavoidable, unprecedented demands for integration, coordination and regulation of society, and unavoidable demands for and expectations of security and fulfillment through autonomy at all levels of society. But the social complexity that elicits these demands is not comprehensible or containable through the conventional application of the dominant mythology or its epistemology that constructs our social reality. Also inadequate are our disjointed legitimating values that predate a world of interlocked processes. Nor is there leadership and citizenship that is aware of, and skilled in, coping with the powerful unconsciously driven responses elicited by the threats to self-images of competence that these demands convey. Consequently, we lack the norms and processes for governance appropriate for meeting either of these demands, much less for synthesizing them. Nor is there available an appropriate mythology which would quickly and easily be widely subscribed to. This in part because our modes of child-raising and education reinforce the dominant myth and are reinforced by it. Add to all this that our chief mode of influencing (aside from coercion) is through language and language is now understood as ungroundable in "objective reality."

Among the fragmented responses these accumulating discontinuities will elicit are those that deny, or seek to deny, all this by recourse to forecasts and planning for the purpose of regaining control or at least providing a coherent context as prelude to regaining control. But these aspirations are very likely to be frustrated in the large even when there are temporary, local successes. Their destiny will much more often be attenuation and dissolution in the cross currents and counterforces that are deaf to, uncomprehending of, or unable to discriminate among the cacophony of messages glutting their parochial perceptual and operational boundaries.

In this situation, is there a utilitarian role or an ethical role, beyond ritual roles and futile outcomes, for forecasting and planning?

Forecasting and Planning in the Midst of Incoherency

GIVEN mounting evidence of societal disarray and lack of success in significantly reducing incoherency, it occasionally may become more acceptable, even good politics, to concede this in public and make a pronouncement such as the following, "We really don't know where we are on this matter or what will work for sure. We must discover and rediscover what questions are useful to ask and what approaches we might experiment with. Therefore, we must become a learning organization (institution, etc.). Rather than deny or project our troubles on the wrong 'causes' or hide our uncertainties, we must use them vigorously as the means for designing error-detecting and error-correcting societal processes." This kind of pronouncement becomes possible because not all those whose self-image is threatened become subject to the psychodynamics of denial or projection. And not all who do succumb are threatened into that state by the same enormities.

Within this perspective, as I have developed it at length elsewhere[30], planning becomes the pedagogy for social learning. Forecasts are integral to this purpose, as an especially rich source of specifiable uncertainties. Among these uncertainties are assumptions about the dynamics of social change, the validity of data, and the consequences of ambiguities in the choice of categories for conceptualizing and of words for conveying the story told. In this perspective, both long range planning and crisis management are means for learning what can be planned and coped with in crises under what circumstances.

The learning curve here for planning-as-learning will be a very shallow slope with many valleys. It can hardly be otherwise given its dependence, at least to begin with, on myth, epistemology and language that will often detour the enterprise. Many traumatic events as well as powerfully salutary ones will intervene, disrupting the slope of the learning curve. It is from these events, in unpredictable ways, that new social constructions of reality will emerge as humans attempt to make sense of what has happened to them. There is no knowing what these new myth(s) might be, emerging, as they seem to, from the unconscious and finding their basic appeal there. What will require fresh interpretation will depend on what events disrupt the social reality constructed by the current myth. It is from such incoherent sources that a new coherence might arise.

Meantime, the perspective offered here—planning as the pedagogy for social learning—has the potential for helping planners, their clients, the recipients of the consequences of plans-in-action, and the creators of forecasts to be self-conscious enough and humble enough to recognize that all are explorers in a strange place that bears a dismaying resemblance to the Tower of Babel.

I am grateful to the Esalen Institute for its continuing support of the Group on Appropriate Governance and to its members: Walter Anderson, Lynton Caldwell, Napier Collyns, JohnFobes, Mary

Jones, Douglas Lea, Brian Murphy, PatOphuls, Elsa Porter, and Steven Waldhorn. All have contributed to my thinking as expressed here but I am responsible for the outcome.

Notes and References

1   Michael, D., With Both Feet Planted Firmly in Mid-air: Reflections on Thinking About the Future, *Futures,* 17, 2, 94-103, 1985.

2   Michael, D., The Futurist Tells Stories. In *What I Have Learned: Thinking About the Future*, Marien, M., and Jennings, L., eds., Greenwood Press, Westport, Conn., 1987.

3   Michael, D., *On Learning to Plan — and Planning to Learn,* Jossey-Bass, San Francisco, 1973.

4   Berger, P., and Luckmann, T., *The Social Construction of Reality,* Harper and Row, New York, 1970.

5   Crowe, B., The Tragedy of the Commons Revisited, *Science* 166, 1103-1107, Nov. 1969.

6   *The Public Interest,* special issue on The Crisis in Economic Theory, 1980.

7   Polanyi, M., *The Tacit Dimension,* Doubleday, New York, 1966.

8   Cochran, N., Society as Emergent and More than Rational: An Essay on the Inappropriateness of Program Evaluation, *Policy Sciences,* 12, 113-129, 1980.

9   Unger, R., *Knowledge and Politics,* Free Press, New York, 1975.

10   Eagleton, T., *Literary Theory,* University of Minnesota Press, Minneapolis, 1983.

11   Gergen, K., The Social Constructionist Movement in Modern Psychology, *American Psychologist,* 40, 3, 266 275, 1985.

12   Lakoff, G., *Women, Fire and Dangerous Things: What Categories Reveal About the Mind,* University of Chicago, Chicago, 1987.

13   Lakoff, G., and Johnson, M., *Metaphors We Live By,* University of Chicago, Chicago, 1980.

14   Van Glasersfeld, E., An Introduction to Radical Constructivism, in *The Invented Reality,* Wutzlawick, P., ed., Norton, New York, 1984.

15   Rittel, H., and Webber, M., Dilemmas in a General Theory of Planning, *Policy Sciences,* 4, 155-169, 1973.

16   Churchman, C. W., *Challenge to Reason,* McGraw-Hill, New York, 1968.

17   Michael, D., Neither Hierarchy nor Anarchy: Notes on Norms for Governance in a Systemic World, in *Rethinking Liberalism,* Anderson, Walter T., ed., Avon, New York, 1983.

18   Dror, Y., *Policy Making Under Adversity,* Transaction Books, New Brunswick, 1986.

19   Riedl, R., The Consequences of Causal Thinking, in *The Invented Reality,* Wutzlawick, P., ed., Norton, New York, 1984.

20   MacIntyre, A., *After Virtue,* University of Notre Dame, Notre Dame, Ind., 1984.

21   Bateson, G., *Steps to an Ecology of Mind,* Ballantine, New York, 1972.

22   Neumann, E., *Depth Psychology and a New Ethic,* Harper Torchbooks, New York, 1973.

23   Michael, D., and Anderson, W. T., Norms in Conflict and Confusion: Six Stories in Search of an Author, *Technological Forecasting and Social Change,* 31, 2, 107 116, 198.

24   Vickers, G., *The Art of Judgment,* Basic Books, New York, 1965.

25   Linstone, H., et al., The Multiple Perspective Concept, *Technological Forecasting and Social Change,* 20: 275-325, 1981.

26   Miller, A., *Prisoners of Childhood,* Basic Books, New York, 1981.

27   Postman, N., *Amusing Ourselves to Death,* Penguin, New York, 1985.

28   Konner, M., *The Tangled Wing,* Holt, Rinehart, and Winston, New York, 1982.

29   Michael, D., Reason's Shadow: Notes on the Psychodynamics of Obstruction, *Technological Forecasting & Social Change,* 26, 2, 149-153, 1984.

30   Michael, D., *On Learning to Plan—and Planning to Learn,* Jossey-Bass, San Francisco, 1973.

31. Schuman, H. and Scott, J., Problems in the Use of Survey Questions to Measure Public Opinion, *Science,* 236, 957-959, 22 May, 1987.

32. Rosenbaum, R., *Manhattan Passions,* Penguin, New York, 1987.

With Both Feet Planted Firmly in Mid-Air

Reflections on Thinking about the Future

How is it that, when I reflect on over 23 years of sharing thoughts about the future, I really cannot convince myself that I know why I was right sometimes and wrong other times? Indeed, often I cannot clearly decide whether I have been right or wrong! Inadequate documentation contributes to this but there are other far more profound reasons for my retrospective malaise. What follows recounts some of what I have learned about thinking about the future and about the appropriate use of such thoughts. In 1963 I wrote:

> "[Thinking about the future] is not a scientific exercise based on consistent theory and heavily documented by field studies and laboratory research. No such theory exists for describing our society accurately—much less for predicting changes in it... Data are by no means trivial but in themselves they are seldom uniquely interpretable in terms of the range of conditions explored ..."[1]

Today, as then, all we have are endless fragments of theory that "account" for bits and pieces of individual, organizational, and economic behavior. But we have no overarching or truly interconnecting theories, especially none that accounts for human behavior in turbulent times.[2] Economic theory is an acknowledged shambles.[3] Social and psychological theories are so inept that their formal status in political rhetoric is nil and, with a few notable exceptions, their uses in the planning and governance processes are more relegated to appendixes than to basic designs and programmes.[4] Most dismaying, even when we think we know the "true" explanation and have an ideal programme for overcoming or attaining a state of affairs, we do not have formal theory indicating how to implement it.[5] That we are unable to correctly predict birthrates embarrassingly epitomizes our ignorance about the interconnectedness of micro and macro processes in the human realm.

It has become increasingly clear to me that overcoming the footless status of futures studies is a far deeper problem than that of closing the gap between data and theory about human behavior in turbulent times. At root the problem is epistemological.[6]

Epistemological Problem in Futures Studies

To begin with, we simply have no way of resolving through cause-effect concepts "the great man in history question": do great men (or events) make history or does history make great men? All futures studies embody this epistemological fog wherein stumble ghostly images about the "momentum" of social "forces" and about the timing and magnitude of shifts in "direction" introduced by persons or events.

If one subscribes, as I do, to Polanyi's arguments, creative human activities have an emergent quality: the "whole" is unpredictably "greater" than the sum of the parts.[7] This seems obvious in the conduct of art, science and politics, and in interpersonal relations. One cannot predict a new theory or art form, nor new political and personal developments from what has gone before. Nor can one predict the consequences of predictions about consequences.[8] After the new state of affairs has emerged interpretations arise that purport to relate causes and effects so as to connect the new condition to what preceded it. But *not* before.

What is more, events, treated as causes or effects, are discrete only if we do not examine them too closely. We choose to identify the beginnings and endings of events by one or another habitual, mythical or professional convention. But everything we experience, especially in an information-dense world, tells us that, individually and collectively, the human condition is overdetermined: everything causes, effects, and is part of, everything else and, in turbulent situations, sensitivity analysis can only refer to a fragment of a moot reality and it may well have already changed.[9] Whatever their individual limitations, the endless proliferation of contending fragments of explanation and the multiple levels of analysis and synthesis they imply amply attest to multiple "causality" and "effects" when it comes to the human condition.

In this regard a fundamental insight for me has been— there are *many* pasts.[10] Alternative choices of events, time periods, interpretations and intentions provide unnumbered ways to link past events to a present. And there are unnumbered ways of putting together the present, i.e. what is "really" happening and what is "really" important. Since the present is always constructed out of a presumed past, I have learned that thoughts about the future derive from preferred constructions of the present and of the past. These constructions are preferred because they are deemed "fitting" in that they seem, according to the prevailing social construction of reality and its cultural norms, to be sensible, familiar, logical, authoritative, or otherwise acceptable beause one has participated in their creation. To be sure, wild cards are included in some thinking about the future, but it is not an accident that such events are suffused with the unacceptability that accompanies the semantics of "wild".[11]

Since multiple pasts and presents make it impossible to bound events definitively as the "containers" of causes and effects, futures forecasts become questionable with regard to what is becoming what out of what. However, fuzzy realities elicit psychological and ideological discomfort: few will create or respond to such future descriptions. Instead, we arbitrarily and habitually (i.e. fittingly) perceive the world as strings of discrete events delineated by anticipatory and retrospective expectations about what "is" an event. We construct (not necessarily consciously) our reality, and then construct our response to that construction—and so on into the future.[12] This is an aesthetic enterprise more than a logical one, even though some techniques used to further the aesthetic endeavour use logic, words etc.[13]

The pronouncements of experts are useful, when thinking about the future, not because their information is based on esoteric and valid knowledge about social change, though that occasionally may be so (but how is one to know?), but because, by virtue of the authority with which they are endowed, i.e. as *experts,* they are able to influence the definition of social reality others hold. Their expertness resides not in a prescience their logic engenders but in the "psychologic" that logic activates: the *authority* of logic and, therefore, of the expert as a practitioner of logic, is what carries weight. This source of authority legitimizes the stories they tell. But the source also tends to subvert the storytellers' own recognition that they are telling stories. Their own belief in their authority, i.e. the authority of logic, leads them to believe they are doing something very different from "merely" telling stories.

Over the years these insights and learnings have led me less and less to the *doing* of futures studies and more and more to questions and understandings regarding the *functions* futures studies perform, or could perform.

Role of Values and Beliefs

As I describe what I have observed about some functions served by futures studies and why are they used or not used, I must first acknowledge that the categories and processes which I describe imply a theory of social change and stasis only some of which is apparent to me. My comments about the epistemological and theoretical footlessness of futures studies also apply to my observations.

I emphasize some less well recognized, though nevertheless crucial ways in which thinking about the future affects individuals as individuals and as members of groups, as participants in organizations and in society. Futures studies serve other functions too but they are better understood or at least more acknowledged than those served at the all important individual level.

I believe that all who create and use thinking about the future do so on the bases of values and myths about what is real, valuable and meaningful. Whether a future study is used, misused or ignored, depends on the producers' and consumers', or anticonsumers', values and beliefs both as these express themselves consciously and through unconscious psychodynamic processes. I have come to believe that self-consciousness about these extra-rational—and sometimes irrational—contributions is fundamental for more effective creation and use of futures studies that are intended to encourage a humane world. How these extra-rational and irrational factors affect the creation and use of futures studies is now my preoccupation.

In the face of imposing intimations of a turbulent and problematic future, the existence of a future study, the very fact that one can be done, provides a kind of comforting talisman, a protection against the unknown. The study comforts by carrying into the future meaning based on what is supposedly happening *now* by using words and concepts that reinforce fitting images in today's society, words such as "economic", "age distribution", "growth rate", "corporation", "national security", "self-interest", "profit", "technology". These ideas, these words, just because they are familiar, offer a comforting sense that, indeed, the map *is* the territory—that behind

all the current turbulence there are real, enduring processes and circumstances at work that can be counted on into the future. For those so moved, it can then seem plausible that the future can be controlled. Consequently this anticipation bolsters a sense of self-confidence.

This sense is further reinforced through the "fitting" methodologies often used to create futures studies—logical process involving mathematics, models, data, numbers, graphs etc. There is also "expert" input which implies control over the subject matter which, in keeping with the dominant Western mythology of the past 300 years, implies the promise of control over events.

That the consumer of futures studies is able to commandeer the combined resources of logic and expertise itself engenders a comforting sense of being in control thereby reducing anxiety about the unknown future.

Commissioners of futures studies are also comforted and reinforced in their sense of competence because they see themselves doing what *rational* persons *ought* to do, i.e. use logic and expertise to solve a problem. Of course, this implied rationality also comforts some of those who are dependent on the actions of the futures studies' sponsors. (Note that in other times, even as today, leaders and their followers were comforted and confirmed in their sense of competence when preparing for the future by doing such fitting things as praying, giving valuables to their "church", doing good deeds etc. Faith, rather than rational procedures, provided protection from the unknown. Today, politics is a popular means for seeking protection from an unknown future.[14])

These satisfactions provided by futures studies typically accompany ritual affirmations of a culture's mythology. This does not make these ritual acts and their satisfactions bad or wrong. Rituals contribute essential stabilities to society. Of exceeding importance, to the extent that rituals comfort and affirm, they encourage conduct compatible with them.

Thus we have a situation in which extra-rational norms and sometimes irrational needs encourage rational behavior. And all this pertains, too, to the functions thinking about the future perform for those who create the futures studies.

In addition to these satisfactions there are other rewards for people who create futures studies. Doing so encourages the belief that one is influential, making a difference, being socially potent and powerful. These beliefs may be justified or they may well be demolished when nothing happens to the product, or if it is misused. But while his or her work is underway, I have yet to meet a "futurist" who didn't feel socially significant and personally vitalized by visions of potential effect amplified by the perceived status of the study commissioners. Often enough these beliefs and visions are inflated by the promotional exertions of authors, organizations, and publishers competing for the rewards of profit and status bestowed by growing numbers of consumers of thoughts about the future.[15]

I have also learned that, much more often than not, futures studies increase discomfort because they expose the recipient to the problematical ramifications of the future. Ambiguity and uncertainty more typically result in anxiety and feelings of role impotency or loss of control. In turn, this state of mind activates psychodynamic responses that are not socially constructive.[16] One such response is to fix on or promulgate one or another future that reduces anxiety by gratuitously avoiding or deprecating the ambiguity and uncertainty—what is called "denial" in the psychodynamic realm.

To be sure, other motives, not all of them unconscious, contribute to these responses. Seldom are they exclusively the consequences of denial: earlier I described human behavior as overdetermined. But many experiences, discussions and probings convince me that futures studies often elicit such unconscious psychodynamic processes. When confronted with the ambiguity and uncertainty which is the message of many futures studies, these processes serve to protect one's image of oneself as a capable person able to control the circumstances for which one is responsible.

Thus, we now have some futurists and their followers proclaiming that we are at a stage where, whether it be the result of evolution or Ilya Prigogine's dissipative structures, we will inevitably emerge into a transformed, better world. That not all turbulence results in higher order systems, that legions of dead species once were vigorous, that denial is a frequent psychodynamic response to anxiety-provoking information—all are overlooked by believers unable to live with more problematic and threatening futures.

Thus, too, we have futurists and their followers who deny that there is anything seriously wrong with the world, that technology, good management and the operation of immutable laws of economics will straighten out present kinks and reward present purposes, and that those who claim otherwise are gloom-and-doomers possessed of a state of mind that smacks of sin (and might even be unpatriotic).

Of course, these two groups of futurists do not by any means exhaust the class. Many of us are able to steer a course between these extremes or navigate in different waters making less threat-denying contributions to our clients' and audience's perspectives, anxieties and enthusiasms.

I have learned that futures studies also elicit psychodynamic processes because they challenge the status quo regarding what is being done, how it is being done, and whether to continue a course of action even if it is now rewarding. In 1973 I began emphasizing that one of the chief contributions of futures studies is to temper our satisfactions with how far we have come by exposing how far we have yet to go, thereby drawing attention to the ethical and operational sufficiency of present actions and policies.[17]

However, each of us harbours conflicting values, which our unconscious and our culture help us avoid recognizing most of the time. Therefore, a communication that, on the one hand,

may well heighten one's anxiety over uncertainty about
which future will eventuate and, on the other, heightens
one's anxiety about where one stands ethically with regard to
those futures, is likely to elicit strong emotional responses.
While futures studies can enlarge the sense of the variety of
win-win opportunities perhaps residing in futures, for many
they threaten to raise acutely discomforting issues about
"What am I entitled to?". In response there is anger, fear,
denial—rejection of the study.

The complex and unavoidable interplay of rewards
and threats with which futures studies face their creators
and consumers leads me to see the functions they serve
for the individual and the responses they elicit as those
accomplished by *storytelling,* that age-old device by which
humans have inspired, influenced and engaged each other.

The Futurist as Storyteller

In what follows, I recognize that futures studies styled
as scenarios embody at their best much of what I shall
urge.[18] But even scenarios seldom take all the advantages
of storytelling that are available to them. In what follows,
my intent is to tell a story within a story, so to speak, not to
establish the logic and norms for doing so.

Nor am I demeaning the usefulness or appropriateness
of telling some stories about the future in the style of a
technical report, with its logical and normative constraints.
These are not necessarily cynical devices for misleading
anyone about the truth any more than is a story about human
reality told in the sonnet form or painted impressionistically.
These are the chosen methodological constraints within
which the artist creates realities. The same holds for
thinking about the future presented in the form of a story
expressed within the constraints of a technical, logical study.
But what is being *told* is still a story and it could be a richer
story if it were recognized and accepted as such. Answers

to the question, "What does the future hold?", that are couched exclusively in rational terms or legitimated in such terms are, at best, only partially satisfying because even the most logical person is only so in part. Here lies a large current limitation in the appeal of serious futures studies in contrast to journalistic exercises which, while substantively questionable, appeal because they are emotionally satisfying. However, *their* limitations are seldom recognized by their enthusiastic readers.

All worthy stories are first and foremost occasions, mirrors and contexts for learning about self by drawing one both inwards and outwards, by expanding one's sense of the plausible. By learning about self one learns about others, for one always sees others through oneself. Thoughts about the future, by the very expansion of context they provide, offer their audience a larger mirror for viewing themselves—a larger mirror, then, for viewing the world and their part in it. Accepted as a story, the range of what is "fitting" can be enlarged because a story need not be constrained by the canons of fittingness that apply  when a communication is treated as if it were exclusively an objective report undergirded with the theory and bolstered by data.

Methodological injunctions

Three methodological injunctions emerge from this vision of the competent and responsible teller of stories about futures. First, shared thoughts about the future ought to include the acknowledgment that, as with the multiple and problematic nature of the futures explored, so too with descriptions and interpretations of the putative past and present from which the futures derive.

Second, shared thoughts about the future ought to be accompanied by an explicit theory about the processes of social change sufficiently detailed so the futures described can be derived from it. If there is no such explicit speculative or tested theory, this ought to be acknowledged. Then both producer and consumer of the story can be more alert to the nature of the tacit and possibly questionable assumptions they hold regarding social change and human nature.

In urging these alternative explicit stances I do not deprecate the contribution of those talented storytellers about futures who sometimes know without knowing how they know—a state of mind the renowned physical scientist and philosopher, Michael Polanyi, used as the basis for elaborating his ideas concerning emergence.[19] I would argue only that the creator of such a futures study is obligated to share the fact of this mind-state with the consumer so that both can make the most imaginative use of a story built in part or wholly on intuitions.

Third, all involved should be vigorously aware that thoughts about the future unavoidably engage both constructive and destructive unconscious needs and images that influence conscious evaluations of purpose and pragmatism. Thereby, these unconscious contributions critically affect the destiny of the futures study. Collusion in the dangerous illusion that one's beliefs and choices can be determined exclusively by rational considerations will gratuitously defeat worthy intentions.[20]

Crucial morals

A worthy and well-told story always implies a moral and stories about the future are especially well suited to convey some crucial morals. One moral meeting emphasis is that the nature of the future world will be an expression of emotions at least as much as of rational deliberations, programmes and practices.

Emotions are critical to what happens—both those emotions driving creativity and reason, aspiration, power, greed and the will to control; and those emotions struggling with the existential questions of being human. As Seymour Sarson summarizes them, they are: "How to dilute the individual's sense of aloneness in the world; how to engender and maintain a sense of community; and how to justify living even though one will die."[21]

Another moral would have it that the future is this splintered civilization's most available and useful context in which to face the personal question: what it is worthwhile to be and to do.

It is not enough to share thoughts about the future restricted to a description of the costs and benefits of introducing one or another new technology, policy or procedure to better realize the intentions of a public or private organization. Somewhere in the process the recipients of the study should be inspired to ask themselves, "What is it all for? Why give thought to the future? Surely not just for profits, or jobs, or the next election or budget hearing. These are very important, of course, but, really, what is it all for? Why am I doing what I am?". If stories about possible futures do not elicit such questions and reflection, where will they come from? And who better to brood on these questions than those who commission or must respond to these thoughts about the future?

Yet another moral: in an uncertain turbulent world, beset with such heavy burdens and challenges as we face, a precondition for a humane future—perhaps for any future at all—is that those who create and use futures studies become compassionate learners. By compassion I mean recognizing that:

(1) In the face of crucial issues nobody, including oneself, really knows what they are doing, certainly not in terms of the *consequences* of their acts;

(2) everyone is, to some profound degree, living in illusions, believing in the "factness" of what comprises their world instead of recognizing that we live in an arbitrarily, though usually not consciously, *constructed* social reality; and

(3) everyone is in one way or another struggling to cope with three existential circumstances that Sarason emphasizes. This means, then, that everyone needs all the clarity they can muster, regarding their ignorance and finiteness, and all the support they can obtain in order to face the upsetting implications of what their clarity reveals to them. A compassionate person is one who, by virtue of accepting this situation, can provide others as well as self with such support.[22]

Well-told stories about futures can hardly avoid emphasizing the moral that resilient participation will require persons and organizations always to be seeking to learn what are the appropriate questions to ask about a changing and turbulent world and to learn *how* to discover and evaluate temporary "answers". Acknowledging and experiencing the personal and organizational life of the learner depends on being open to unfamiliar ideas and experiences and on being increasingly interdependent. Both requirements demand exceptional degrees of vulnerability. But being vulnerable can lead to a humane world only if the norms of compassion are practised. Otherwise, those willing to risk a learning stance will be destroyed by the power hungry and hostile. Learning how to establish such norms will be as difficult as it is unavoidable and this, too, becomes a moral of futures stories.[23]

There is one more moral to the story I am telling here and to the stories I propose be told by futures studies. I have learned that all these morals hold as well for the *authors* of futures stories. We are not outside the story we tell: each of us is part of the story. Each must be a quester after existential meaning, vulnerable, uncertain, and ethically concerned about what happens to our thoughts about the future since, if they are used, they will affect the future we are telling stories about.

The Delphic injunction, "Know thyself", is the most essential of all conditions for meaningful and responsible engagement when thinking about the future, for finding one's way among the claims, distortions, feelings and fantasies that each of us harbours in our unconscious. Constructive and destructive unconscious needs drive "futurists"—myself included—as well as the consumers of futures studies. To be indifferent to the fact or impact of these circumstances in ourselves is to forgo crucial insights into our functions and responsibilities as the creators of futures studies.

An Unfolding Story...

WHAT I've learned about thinking about the future is, of course, not the whole story. There are always stories within stories that, if told in the words of another storyteller, could emerge and take over. And there are stories that surround any given story which, when told, change the meaning of the story within. This is life and it is precisely the value of a story, acknowledged as such: it draws much more out of the audience and out of the world than does a story presented as something else—as a "logical", "scientific", "value-free" report, for example. So too herein.

Therefore I don't doubt that telling this story about what I have learned about the story telling we call thinking about the future, will change the story I tell... some time in the future.

Notes and References

1   D. Michael, *The Next Generation: Prospects Ahead for the Youth of Today and Tomorrow* (New York, Random House, 1965).

2   If one needs any evidence that it is beyond our conceptual capabilities to cohere all the different worldviews, preoccupations, reports, forecasts etc. into anything remotely resembling a unified picture from which rational encompassing interpretations and decisions can be made, let him or her peruse any edition of *Future Survey*. The issue of 6 (4), April 1984 provides an especially representative sample of the swamp of ideas into which we are sinking ever deeper—with the help of the information revolution (about which there are, in this edition, two important critiques reviewed by the editor).

3   Whole issue, "The crisis in economic theory", *The Public Interest*, special edition, 1980; N. Georgescue-Rogan, *The Entropy Law and the Economic Process* (Cambridge, Harvard University Press, 1971); V. Leontief, "Academic economics", *Science*, 217, July 1982, pages 104-107; H. Striner, *Regaining the Lead* (New York, Praeger, 1984).

4   A. Mazur, "Evaluating the social sciences", *Science*, 216, May 1981, page 875; S. Koch, "The nature and limits of psychological knowledge", *American Psychologist*, 36 (3), March 1981, pages 257-269.

5   H. Rittel and M. Webber, "Dilemmas in a general theory of planning", *Policy Sciences, 4*, 1973, pages 155-169.

6   R. Unger, Knowledge and Politics (New York, Free Press, 1975); I. Mitroff and R. Killman, *Methodological Approaches to Social Science* (San Francisco, Jossey-Bass, 1978).

7   M. Polanyi, *The Tacit Dimension* (New York, Doubleday, 1966).

8   N. Cochran, "Society as emergent and more than rational: an essay on the inappropriateness of program evaluation", Policy Sciences, 12, 1980, pages 113-129.

9   R. Bauer *et al, Second Order Consequences: A Methodological Essay on the Impact of Technology* (Cambridge, MIT Press, 1969).

10 No other mode of cognitive exposure has so informed me of my ignorance about past, present and future, and my epistemological footlessness, as has exposure to histories of ideas and societal change. This continues to be a source of dismaying and exciting shocks to my emotions as well as to my intellect. Most informative for me, regarding many issues I am exploring here, is H. Arendt, *The Human Condition* (Garden City, Doubleday, 1958). Also high on the list are: H. David, "Assumptions about man and society and historical constructs in futures research", *Futures, 2 (3)*, 1970; A. Toynbee, *A Study of History* (New York, McGraw Hill, 1972); F. Wyatt, "The reconstruction of the individual and of the collective past", in R. White, ed, *The Study of Lives* (New York, Atherton Press, 1963).

11 Here are three personal examples of different kinds of unfittingness: (1) the then president of the Brookings Institution was very unhappy about the report I prepared under its auspices for NASA (D. Michael, *Proposed Studies on the Implications of Peaceful Space Activities for Human Affairs* (Washington, DC, Brookings Institution, 1965), because I discoursed on the implications of discovering intelligent extraterrestrial life. Most unfitting, by Brookings standards of respectability; (2) some criticized my *The Next Generation, op cit*, reference 1, because I did not predict the future but instead suggested that things could go in different ways. A futures approach was not as fitting then as it is now; (3) in the 1960s it was fitting to speculate on the longer-run implications of automation and computers, especially the impacts on the workforce and privacy (see D. Michael, *Cybernation: The Silent Conquest* [Santa Barbara, Center for the Study of Democratic Institutions, 1962]). In the 1970s there were fitting ways to deprecate the issue and it essentially disappearing from futures speculations. Now, of course, the topic is real and it is hot... but as if the thinking of the 1960s never happened.

12 K. Mannheim, *Man and Society in an Age of Reconstruction*, Edward Shils, trans (London, Routledge and Kegan Paul); M. Novak, *The Experiences of Nothingness* (New York, Harper and Row, 1970); P. Berger and T. Luckmann, *The Social Construction of Reality* (Garden City, Doubleday, 1964); G. Vickers, *The Art of Judgment* (New York, Basic Books, 1965).

13 D. Michael, "Technology assessment in an emerging world", *Technological Forecasting and Social Change*, 11 (1), February 1978, pages 189-195.

14 C. West Churchman, *The Systems Approach and its Enemies* (New York, Basic Books, 1979).

15 D. Michael, *The Unprepared Society: Planning for a Precarious Future* (New York, Basic Books, 1968), Chapter I.

16   D. Michael, "Reason's shadow: notes on the psychodynamics of obstruction", *Technological Forecasting and Social Change*, 26 (2), September 1984, pages 149-153.

17   D. Michael, *On Learning to Plan—and Planning to Learn* (San Francisco, Jossey-Bass, 1973).

18   P. Hawken, J. Ogilvy, P. Schwarts, *Seven Tomorrows* (New York, Bantam, 1982).

19   Polanyi, op cit, reference 7.

20   D. Michael, "Ritualized rationality and arms control", *Bulletin af the Atomic Scientists*, 17 (1), February 1961, pages 71-73.

21   S. Sarason, "The nature of problem solving in social action", *American Psychologist*, April 1978, pages 370-380.

22   D. Michael, "Learning from the future", World Future Society Bulletin, 12 (4), July-August 1979, pages 1-5.

23   That the human implications for the users of futures thinking have yet to be appreciated is easily evidenced by the number of organizations that apply some thinking about the future to their planning and strategy activities but then go on to perform in the same managerial style as before. See W. Halal, "Strategic management: the state of the art and beyond", *Technological Forecasting and Social Change, 25* (3), May 1984, pages 239-261. I began writing about this interconnection in op cit, references 15 and 17, but it is only recently that multiple circumstances (in their usual overdetermined way) have begun to encourage some efforts to humanize management that truly responds to the story told in some futures thinking.

LEADERSHIP'S SHADOW:
THE DILEMMA OF DENIAL

WHAT follows is an argument with myself, albeit a polemic too. But as with many thoughtful arguments, there is no last word: I am not sure where I come out. Why do I presume, then, to make a claim on the reader's time and effort? Because in the realm of issues regarding the conduct of governance in open societies (and closed ones, for that matter) I know of none more in need of examination precisely because, by its very nature, it has not had the attention it deserves. Lacking that attention, any conclusions would be premature. Lacking that attention, I think we are and will be in deep, deep trouble—probably.

The Threat

ARGUABLY, the most profound threat to the development of a planetary civilization is the inability of leaders to admit that there are fundamental circumstances with which we must deal that cannot be acknowledged.[1] In part this is because to do so would require confessing that, as of now, we do not know how to deal with them. What is more, this inability to acknowledge this mute state of affairs is also part of the situation that cannot be acknowledged. This malady is not a new situation. In private, some public figures are able to admit this within their realms of knowledgeability. But most assuredly, *not* in public. Nor do most public figures possess the strength of character to do this. Many cannot or will not face this dilemma; that dealing with the underlying threats to our civilization requires acknowledging them, and such acknowledgment, because it would threaten so many in so many ways, would be rejected and denied, as would the bearer of the bad news, the Leader. As Freud observed, the first thing that is denied is the fact of denial as a pervasive psychological condition.

Meanwhile, societal problems collide, pile up and gridlock in ever more complex disarray, and the more complex and disarrayed the situation becomes, the less possible it becomes for leaders to acknowledge that this is so. For to do so would be to admit that they do not understand the complexity and, not understanding it, do not really know what to do about it. This is not what leaders expect of themselves, nor is it what those people want to hear who look to them for the psychological support a leader is expected to supply. Indeed, citizens faced with spiralling uncertainty and turbulence may well turn to another leader who claims to understand the situation and to know what must be done to solve it.

How shall I go about explicating this depressing topic? Within the ambit of this essay, I can only outline it, and in doing so, surely over generalize. Exceptions need to be delineated and qualifications appended in order to refine the argument. But the exceptions and qualifications do not alter the fundamental point. First, I describe some underlying circumstances, the acknowledgment of which is essentially taboo in public discourse (though not so completely in specialized realms of thought disconnected from public action, such as this one). Next I discuss why so often we are unable to face these matters. Finally, I examine the putative feasibility of ways out of the impasse.

Before doing so, I shall anticipate a likely question from the reader: "Why undertake such a distasteful, discouraging exercise? Why be so pessimistic? Don't we need, instead, optimistic visions, the pursuit of which may lead to their realization?". I turn to hope instead of optimism, that state of mind that wills going on seeking betterment in the face of evil and confusion without any gratuitous belief that the effort will succeed. To avoid looking carefully at the shadow side of the human condition is to trivialize it and thereby to reduce the chances of discovering a way out of this deepening mess. It is in this spirit of hope that I undertake the rest of this essay.

Taboo Topics

HERE, then, are some of the circumstances that cannot be publicly acknowledged.

Since there exists no reliable theory of social change under turbulence, we cannot attempt actions knowledgeably or with any honest conviction that what we choose to do is on the right track, or even likely to be so.[2]

Examples of this theoretical groundlessness? We still cannot predict changes in birthrates; ample evidence that we do not know how micro and macro social forces influence each other in this critical area. Nor can we predict radical shifts in public positions such as women's liberation or the ecology movement. Of course, *after* the fact we can contrive an explanation; before the fact we cannot predict the substance and direction of such changes.[3] A third example, almost too obvious to mention, is the increasing evidence that available economic theory cannot accomplish the tasks of interpretation or prediction required of it. At present, it is all bailing wire and Scotch tape.[4] Put bluntly, we do not know where we are going.

Many reasons contribute to this lack of theory about social change. One reason is another taboo topic: the complexity of the human condition is now so great that it is probably incomprehensible.[5] Perhaps that has always been the case; resignation to "God's inscrutable ways" was an earlier way of acknowledging this circumstance. So too was the romantic celebration of the mystery and contingency of human experience. Currently, however, for many, especially those who make decisions affecting the public, such inscrutability is hardly firm ground or consoling.

Another indicator of increasing uncomprehended complexity is provided through the information revolution.

Its outpouring reveals that the more we know, the more we need to know in order to make sense of what we know. To be sure, in many realms of science more information reduces uncertainty. But far more often than not, in the realms of human conduct more information increases uncertainty about what's "out there"—including uncertainty about the reliability and competence of the information sources.

So, not only can we not say with any confidence where we are going, but we do not know what we are talking about. Of course, this cannot be admitted in public! But most people know so little about this complex world that the enormity of our predicament is lost on them. They live in a world perceived through a distorting lens that personalizes societal circumstances and reduces them to simple cause-and-effect sequences. (This is currently evidenced in the USA by the large and admiring consensus that President Reagan was "The Great Communicator". But *what* he communicated was a simple world of conventional wishful thinking, a world that for the most part never existed unalloyed or untarnished. This is *why* it can be communicated: it's simple—resonant with simple minds and simple wishes.)

Socialization and Education

STATED as a topic, our child socialization processes and our approach to education have resulted in a population that, for the most part, are unable and unwilling to think with the subtlety, skill and persistence required of citizens for knowledgeable (rather than ritual) participation in the conduct of democratic governance in a complex and ambiguous world. It is not a matter of whether most people could learn to read with some understanding, do enough arithmetic to balance their home accounts, write simple, coherent paragraphs, or even become modestly computer-literate. They *could*, but far more is required to engage this world knowledgeably: the ability to read, write and discourse habitually in terms of multiple variables, dialectical processes, systems dynamics, both/and instead of either/or logic, and circular instead of linear cause-effect relationships. In the absence of such skills leaders cannot discourse about complexity—even if they wanted to. Also required is at least an understanding of and feeling for the basics of psycho-dynamics as they affect their own behavior and that of others in the public arena.

But to acknowledge these requirements is to risk being branded "elitist", since there is no evident way for this to become the general level of education in the foreseeable future. Most parents and most teachers do not think in these ways, nor do most other adults. If they did, the world of advertising and TV news (from which 71% of the American public get *all* their news information) would go belly-up. And most universities would have to fire most of their faculty members whose thinking outside (and too often within) their specialisms is as lacking in the requisite skills as the rest of the population, as the goings-on at most faculty meetings demonstrate.

The sophisticated thinking modes required surely depend in part on the early cultivation of mind and spirit. Under current circumstances, cultivating those skills would further separate most children from most parents, parents who do not think in these ways, and parents who lack the emotional maturity to support their offspring as they move away from their outmoded conceptual world.

Inept child education is one contributor to the incapacity of most to think competently. The indictment is broader, however, and reveals another circumstance that cannot be admitted publicly: the state of this world suggests that many, many parents at all socioeconomic levels—it is not simply a matter of economic deprivation—make poor or negative contributions to the shaping of a next generation able to grow into the emotionally mature, cognitively competent, socially responsible adulthood crucial for attaining and maintaining a complex, interdependent and humane world. Parents do poorly because they themselves lack these attitudes, values and skills, passing on to the next generation the consequences of their own neuroses and counterproductive values and lifestyles.[6] Of course, in an invasive and interdependent world that differs for each generation, the blame does not lie only with parents. My point is that the sacredness of the family and of the belief that parents know best makes it impossible to acknowledge that, for many reasons, many parents seriously damage children's potential, but that there is no reliable, general-purpose substitute for them that can be expected to do a better job.

There is an intriguing parallel in another unadmitted double-bind: the nation state is obsolete as the geopolitical entity for creating a better world, but there is no reliable or acceptable substitute for it. Its traditional virtue has been its ability to protect its citizens from incursions that jeopardize their benefits. But it can no longer protect from weapons or terrorism; from job loss or financial insecurity in an international economy; from toxic substances diffused regionally or planetwide; or from those moral challenges from oppressed segments of humanity that, though distant, can no longer be ignored. But for a public figure to assert that the nation state is an obsolete concept, and that there is no substitute for it, exposes that leader at the very least to accusations of being unpatriotic, of selling out to competitors or enemies. Moreover, revealing the vulnerability of the nation state deprives both the leader and many citizens of a psychological security blanket of great worth—a shared identity and the comfort of believing that the nation state protects them from... whatever.[7]

Unconscious Forces

YET another taboo. Out of ignorance or fear, most of us, including leaders, are unable to acknowledge how profoundly unconscious psychological forces, genetic predispositions and cultural definitions of reality shape how we think, feel and act.[8] These constructive and destructive injunctions usually undergird what we claim we do in the name of logic, decency, or whatever. "Michael's maxim" says that "we choose our social causes in terms of our own psychological needs". Thereby, I am not evaluating the causes. I am asserting that different causes appeal to different individual unconscious forces. Or, that one reads into a cause that which serves one's own psychological needs.

Bertrand Russell and Nietzsche before him observed that appealing to logic (or what passes for logic) is but an elaborate excuse for doing what we *want* to do. To recognize this would profoundly threaten our beliefs about what is necessary for reliable and informed decisions and actions. Many educated people believe that if we understand one another, through conscious reasoning, then we can find a solution to our differences. American culture emphasizes this belief in the dominance of conscious thought in ideas and action, probably more than other societies, but the Western world generally subscribes to this view. In fact, we are all heirs to unrecognized, unconscious forces that express themselves in subtle, and sometimes overwhelming, needs for prestige and power, or to nurture, or to understand, or to dominate, or to submit.

Sometimes, *after the fact*, the contribution of negative unconscious forces is exposed in revelations about a public or private leader's behavior, and sometimes they are open secrets during his or her incumbency. However, it is to the point that, both to protect the incumbent's role and to ensure the continuing acceptability of the reporter of such discomforting information, these topics are functionally taboo. Nevertheless, the implications of the role of the unconscious, or the fact that we are all driven by "daemonic" forces (Rollo May's phrase) for good and evil is, of course, not part of the public evaluation of potential leadership competence. In societies that believe themselves to be rational, few can acknowledge that one's culture protects one from recognizing the force of the unconscious in public affairs by surrounding leaders with symbols of conscious, rational reasoning—data, commissions, reports, debates, treaties etc. To be sure, all these play a part in consciously contending with the power of the unconscious in any group or individual, but "insider" reports provide ample evidence that, to some degree, unconsciously driven hopes, fears, obsessions, prejudices, tantrums and habits carry the day in corporate boardrooms, government offices, and wherever else values, goals and personalities clash or mesh.

Ethics

My last tabooed example infuses all the others and is a consequence of our inability to admit these tabooed circumstances. We have no ethics, nor do we know what the ethics should be, appropriate for making hard choices in a contentious yet *systemic* world—a world where, increasingly, everything is connected to everything else over time as well as space; where the "buck" doesn't stop anywhere; where the consequences of decisions reverberate ever more powerfully because the technologies through which choices are expressed and implemented are ever more powerful.[9]

Our available ethics derive from historic experiences with small, distinct, separate entities—self, family, group, nation—in which "we" and "they" were clearly distinguishable. In the US ethical/legal tradition, one has (in theory at least) the right to do with one's own (including self) what one wants, as long as it does not infringe on another's rights or well-being. But we are now in a world where almost anything one does as a person, group or nation intrudes on others. We are in a world where our ethics still emphasize rights and autonomy, but where the actual circumstances make imperative close attention to obligations and interdependence.

Examples abound: who pays the social bills incurred by farmers or workers subject to a planetary economy, or Third World debtors, or those of a megacorporation whose failure has large social consequences, or for welfare services for illegal immigrants or beggars on the streets, or for cleaning up old toxic dumps? Answering these queries depends on answering, in the old perspective, "Who's to blame?". Blame and reward are determined by where the system's boundaries are set, but we do not know anymore where to set them—in space or time. When the blame is multiple and interdependent, and different depending on the timespan embraced, and when the rewards derived from earlier decisions that now create costs are widely distributed, as they have been—jobs, profits, lower-priced products, convenience, health etc.—then who should gain and who should lose *now*? Consider, too, that if public figures were to acknowledge the imperative need for, and absence of, such a systems ethic, they would also have to acknowledge that their *own* institutions and organizations operate according to an outdated ethic. This would threaten their own status. It also invites confrontation from those who have claimed that this has been the case all along.

What's Going on Here?

Given these circumstances, how to explain the fact of taboo topics in an open society? How can this be, since occasionally, at least in policy-oriented literature[10] and in backroom, hair-down, conversations the taboos are sometimes acknowledged in frustration and despair? Nor is the phenomenon uniquely American; it is characteristic of public and private leadership worldwide.

The first explanation leaders offer is that acknowledging taboos is simply bad politics. To claim that the issues exist, but that as of now, we really don't know what to do about them, guarantees that they will not be attended to; too many, at all levels of society, benefit from ignoring or denying their existence. Moreover, leaders depend heavily on team play to accomplish the big tasks they *can* attempt, as well as the persistent drumfire of more mundane tasks to which they must attend. All are in jeopardy if a leader threatens the image, interests and perspectives of potential allies.

There are many ways to neutralize a leader who attempts to break taboos. A powerful one is for other leaders to assert that he or she is not privy to the really important facts or circumstances and to back this attack with their allied experts. These neutralizing tactics have great appeal for those who, intent on "having it all", do not want to know about, much less wrestle with, the taboos. It is not only other leaders who would destroy the bearer of bad news.[11] Recall the reasons for Socrates' death. Note, too, that David Stockman was widely chastised, and not only by conservatives, for washing the Reagan administration's dirty linen in public. He was seldom commended for revealing how vulnerable and contributive the government can be to duplicitous manoeuvres.

Another reason for the silence: it is a rare leader who is thoughtful and knowledgeable enough and who possesses the psychological maturity to look into the abyss. Most leaders are simply ignorant about the basic issues. They lack the perspectives, knowledge, time and skills; they, too, are the products of a mal-education system. Thereby, they, along with their constituents, customers and peers, lack the incentives to look at the taboos.

Unconscious psychodynamic factors help sustain the taboos. Here I single out the psychodynamic process called "denial".

> "Begin with the fact that each person has an image of him/herself, for the most part unconsciously held or nonverbally felt, that defines for that person, 'This is who I *am*. This is *me*.' Ideas, events or experiences that undermine that image undermine a person's very existence: it is a deep threat to one's very being.[12] As such, it engenders intolerable anxiety. A typical way psychodynamic processes operate to cope with such a threat is to deny its existence. Denial may occur by trivializing the threat so its enormity does not get through consciously. (E.g., the problem really is not that serious or, technology, the play of the market, socialist doctrine, or the forces of transformation will solve the problem is the long run. Or, we can beat them.)
>
> Or denial may operate so that the threat is not consciously noticed or acknowledged. The threat is repressed, transferred to the unconscious where it persists in disguised forms — e.g., as nightmares or displaced onto other less threatening 'objects' such as 'enemies'.
>
> [Now] consider . . . persons whose self-images include the belief that they are highly rational, especially in the face of crises, and powerful (in status and influence), i.e., persons who believe themselves to be competent — a self-image reinforced and sustained by the fact and by selective perceptions of past successes. Face them with the profound threats to their competence posed by the appallingly complex issues [described here] . . . Some . . . avoid the acute anxiety connected with conscious recognition of these

threats to their self-image as rational, powerful, and competent [by repressing into the unconscious what they cannot] afford to face. Thereby, they are able to ignore schemes which require, in order to evaluate and act upon them, that they face directly the threats they are denying. Moreover, by denying the overwhelming seriousness of the issues, they can reject the proposal on the grounds that it is politically infeasible or somebody else's problem. Business as usual, then is sometimes maintained by the psychodynamic process of denial.

... Wouldn't a solution (in contrast to an analysis) reduce the threat conveyed by the issue, and consequently be embraced because it maintains a self-image? Sometimes yes; but other times no. To see the possibilities in the proposed solution it would be necessary *first* to recognize previously denied threatening aspects of the issue. Letting go of a non-threatening viewpoint in order to try a problematic solution appropriate to a threatening viewpoint may entail too much psychological risk."[13]

Given a leader's privileged status, one cannot draw evidence from a therapist's notes, so to speak, but endless anecdotes support the supposition that even leaders are vulnerable to this deeply human tendency.

I want to be clear here. I am not asserting that denial inevitably operates to block the capacity to face fundamental issues, though unconscious forces always play a part, constructively as well as destructively, in everyone's behavior. But it surely plays a part some of the time. When it does, it aids and abets positions espoused by other leaders—positions that recommend not rocking the boat further—especially if it is also believed that the boat (a) is already rocking precariously, or (b) it will settle down if left alone, or (c) that concentrating on current actions will settle it down. And of course denial in some leaders is compatible with ignorance in other leaders and publics.

What Then?

CHANGES do occur. But can they happen—more importantly, can they be *made* to happen—on a scale and depth needed even to hope to deal with the accumulating backlog of gridlocked issues, a backlog *partially* resulting from not admitting their existence? Earlier, I emphasized that there is no widely shared theory of social change under turbulent conditions, adequate for reliably understanding what is happening. So here *I* must avoid tacitly inventing or assuming one. Instead I will speculate, drawing on psychological insights where I can.

Crises and disasters have been the occasion for change. Sometimes, what was taboo regarding the pre-disaster situation becomes acknowledged, and sometimes basic change follows from this. The change-engendering efficacy of such events depends partially on how the occasion is interpreted.[14] World Wars I and II, the Great Depression, and the Holocaust each opened certain conventionally unexamined representations of social reality to questioning and to changes in conduct. Questions regarding the sufficiency of the belief in the civilizing contributions of education and reason, the legitimacy of white colonial goals and norms, the responsibility of government for the welfare of its citizens, and the banality of evil, all emerged as legitimate issues for public examination.

However, it does not follow that crises and disasters invariably lead to the demystification of taboos. Over the reach of history, it seems that the tendency has been to claim that disaster came as the result of deviations from true beliefs and conduct.[15] Systems collapse in turbulence[16] as well as emerge into a new level of stability (a fact apparently lost on those who turn to the work of Prigogine[17] for comfort in these turbulent times).

Sometimes a religion has demystified some taboos. In forwarding its own vision and morality, it exposes its version of the ignorance and corruption hidden in a society's unacknowledged circumstances, or otherwise raises unconventional questions about the way the society works. Recently, in the USA, the Catholic Bishops' Letter in 1986 did this by questioning capitalism's capability to meet human needs.

The worldwide resurgence of religious quests and commitments attests to a deep-lying unease with extant cultures' capability to deal with their underlying problems, even though those turning to new or old religions disagree about what is missing or has gone wrong and what norms and conduct should prevail. Nevertheless, in so doing they sometimes point to otherwise politically taboo topics.

The downside, of course, is that the very needs for assurance and comfort sought through religion are supplied through dogma and rigid norms that run precisely counter to the exploratory stance needed to discover how to cope constructively with the underlying issues. One set of taboos is replaced by another, and all too often, the history of religion is the history of slaughter in the name of truth.

Future Leadership

WHAT about visionary leadership,[18] leadership like that of Mohandas Gandhi, Kemal Ataturk, Peter the Great, Mao Tse-tung, Abraham Lincoln, Winston Churchill, or Martin Luther King, Jr? Could such a leader reveal today's and tomorrow's tabooed circumstances and admit that we have yet to discover how to deal with them, but deal with them we must? Perhaps, but we know reliably very little about the social and psychological dynamics involved. (As for Mikhail Gorbachev, we shall have to wait and see what we learn from his performance.)

Some such leaders arise in response to overt crises, others to widely sensed implicit crises. And surely these are such times. But could such a leader or leaders arise in ever more complexly structured and disordered societies where so many have deeply vested and powerfully held interests in the status quo (more or less) and, thereby, strong unconscious as well as conscious needs to deny the reality of the fundamental unrecognized issues such a leader must point to? Many who would follow would not do so out of a knowledgeable assessment of our complex and uncertain world. Instead, they would transfer to such heroic personages their unrequited infantile needs to be mothered or fathered, to be nurtured and protected.[19] At the extreme, assassination is an all too familiar means for eliminating charismatic leadership that threatens one or another group's interests.

Another situation has arisen since the days of such heroic leaders, itself a manifestation of a fundamental issue confronting open societies: the emergence of single-issue political constituencies and powerful legal and communicative means for imposing one group's interests on another, or at least, obstructing the actions of other special-interest groups ... all legitimated by the idea of participative democracy.

Participative democracy needs information, and the information society provides it in superabundance. Participative democracy needs access, and the expanding information society, aided by the ingenuity of attorneys, provides it. However, the result is an ever deepening set of dilemmas and impasses:

> *"Information cuts both ways and herein lie the dilemmas or paradoxes arising from ever more information created, processed and disseminated by proliferating information technologies. More information can result in more control but it also creates circumstances that reduce or defy control. It clarifies some issues but it obscures and complexifies others. It enlarges the opportunities for participation in decision making and in doing so it both increases and reduces the incentives for adversarial*

confrontations in the courts and on the streets. It brings more ideas into the market place but at the cost of raising the noise level to where nothing can be heard clearly. Unprecedented amounts of information can be brought to bear on issues of policy and action but the persons who must use the information to make decisions become overloaded and everything gets muddled. In some cases one feels more information really gives an understanding of a situation. In more cases more information deepens a feeling of uncertainty. Information gives some ever greater access to a more complex world while condemning others to deeper isolation and alienation. It facilitates the coherence of groups and, at the same time, helps groups to splinter. It can make for both centralization and decentralization of power. In such ways information entices some into ever more demands for information and others to turn away from more information because it upsets habits of mind and action."[20]

But perhaps outspoken leadership arising elsewhere is not impossible? What about the emergence of leadership via grassroot movements? Popular movements in the USA and abroad have occasionally surfaced taboo topics, and by doing so have stimulated changes in laws and conduct. But the nature of the necessary and sufficient conditions for the occurrence of such changes continues to be researched and argued. Our ignorance here is important evidence of the absence of good social change theory. Consider too, that to recruit committed and active memberships, it seems necessary for grassroots movements to assert *the* truth, *the* answers. So, even when they expose one or another otherwise politically taboo topic, their goal—a particular solution to it—is not a sufficient approach to the complexity of the topic. However, charismatic leadership from such convinced and committed sources is obviously comforting for some people. Conceivably such leadership, if not co-opted, could displace established political systems. But its very motivational sources, and the confrontations it would have to defeat, would surely encourage risking the demagogic abyss — substituting one set of taboos for another in the name of truth.

Muddling Through?

WHAT about leaving well enough alone and just muddling through? The proposition begs the question, since "muddling through" implies that we will come out the other side in good shape, comfortably connected with what went before. It assumes we can make it because we always have. In turn, this assumes that what must be muddled through is not essentially different in degree or kind from what was muddled through before. The issues enumerated here make it clear that the tasks of governance and leadership are now and will be fundamentally different from those in the past, in part because muddling through by past and current leadership has helped produce the present gridlock of operational, policy and conceptual predicaments.

The clash of contending conscious and unconscious interests, needs and values will surely continue.[21] Even given time and candid acknowledgments, it will be long before most humans *experience* the generative circumstances — the disasters, accomplishments and conflicts — and learn from them that which might moderate behavior into the compassionate ways needed to live humanely, according to a systems ethic (as discussed above), in an increasingly complex world. That is we *might* interpret our experiences in such ways as to engender values and a psychology that sustains a society of explorers — learners.[22] Such a society would self-consciously question its premises as well as its actions, accept uncertainty, and measure leadership competence at all levels by its capacity to acknowledge ignorance and uncertainty as prerequisites for discovery and change, i.e., as the conditions for learning.[23] But this is an enormous challenge and most of what I have written here argues that realizing a learning society would be an extraordinary accomplishment indeed.

But the accomplishments, conflicts and disasters to come might instead result in the demise of the open society, in a retreat psychologically and politically into isolation from new ideas, in an overwhelming insistence on law and order (accompanied by endless clashes over *whose* law and order). Even now there are many moves in this direction, even as there are many experiments to open societies still further.

But perhaps it isn't necessary that most people deeply understand the world they live in? Perhaps the underlying mess and current ignorance about what to do about it need *not* be acknowledged? Perhaps we can depend on an innate something to bring out the right judgments in the population—the heart's reasons, so to speak? This perennial belief arguably had some validity in simpler days, when the publicly perceived social reality pretty well matched that described by sophisticated observers. But not today or tomorrow! Or, indeed, even yesterday. For example, the constructors of the US Constitution were quite explicit in their understanding that the common good depended on more than an inchoate impulse to do the right thing, to choose the right leaders. It depended on an electorate *educated* in and acting out a commitment to civic virtue.[24]

Hope, Anyone?

WHERE does this leave those of us who have trudged this far into the thicket? Some readers, no doubt, will reject all this as "gloom and doom thinking", as lamentable pessimism. The argument would go that the problems are unacknowledged because they are not real, not because the cost of acknowledging them is too great for a leader to risk. Both contradictory information and a validated model of social change under turbulence being absent, I believe that such rejection is an example of denial —or of sheer ignorance—about the conditions described, about the norms of political conduct, and about the psycho-dynamics of the unconscious in each of us, including leaders. At this stage of my exploration I am led to expect leaders to continue to deny publicly, and often to themselves that, underlying surface conditions, are issues such as those listed here, and that we do not know what to do about them. And I expect most publics will continue to prefer this behavior from their leaders, even to insist on it. Therefore, I also expect the psychological, social and economic costs of the pile-up of interlocked complexities to accelerate. And, as tolerance for these costs evaporates over time, perhaps society will slouch into something quite different and probably very unpleasant, some kind of an updated European 14th century or Japanese 16th and early 17th centuries.[25]

But perhaps a combination of tinkering with the surface of things, forced by contending with grassroots agitation, illuminated by the critical interpretations of some thinkers, and inspired by occasional enlightened and fortunate leaders—so much depends on unanticipated events— together with the extraordinary adaptability of this-species, will result in societies more slowly burdened by deepening costs and, therefore, tolerant enough of them to avoid total collapse from conflict and despair. After all, even today many in the US population (not to say the rest of the world) are victims of one or another combination of drug abuse, incivility, mindless obsessive consumption of entertainment and material goods, white collar and other crimes, child and mate abuse, job vulnerability, ignorance, pervasive uncertainty, anxiety, alienation, emotional immaturity, exploitation and abject poverty. But they do go on living, making what they can of their circumstances.[26] And there are many innovative social experiments and some probing critical commentary forwarded to counter these degraded conditions, to create more enlightened ways of being and doing.

So there are reasons to hope—*not* to be optimistic, but to *hope*. In the first place, for humans to stop hoping is to guarantee both individual and societal premature death. Moreover, given our ignorance, we cannot conclude that nothing can be done. That we do not understand social change under conditions of turbulence is both a compelling reason why leadership denies and remains silent and why we cannot use our current interpretations of what is happening to justify hopelessness. For example, while I do not see how treating the symptoms instead of the disease can cure or even stabilize the patient's condition, neither I nor anyone else can be certain that one or another symptom treatment cannot succeed through some as yet unrecognized or undiscovered societal process.

For example, the very fact that a nation state can no longer protect its citizens from the impacts of environmentally destructive agents, economic forces, ideas, and weapons from outside its boundaries, is nudging nation states into collaborative arrangements that, while engendered by the symptoms, are, willy-nilly, creating a global society unrecognized and certainly not managed as such. Given enough time, and given enough evident support from those who are not leaders, a political atmosphere might emerge here and there that would encourage the kind of leadership and followership necessary in order to face the underlying systemic issues.

Another example: the accumulation of obvious failures of programmes and policies undertaken with assurances from leaders that they would succeed, that they (and their experts) understand what is needed and how to accomplish it, may make it good politics eventually, here and there, for a leader to say out loud, "Those who claim to know what to do are either fools or liars and, by gratuitously claiming certainty about cause and effect, they foreclose experimenting with additional options".

As with the large picture, so too with this essay. There is no way to know beforehand whether this incremental effort matters. But if we are ever to unravel what I believe to be an ever tightening, self-complicating knot, some of whose lineaments I've tried to discern, it will be necessary (though not sufficient) to bring to bear all the understanding we can by acknowledging the intellectual and psychodynamic fix we are in instead of ignoring them in the name of optimism or positive visions.

Notes and References

1   Generally speaking, when I refer to "leaders" I am including those at whatever level, in formal organizations or otherwise, who are looked to for public statements that, by virtue of their leadership role, are expected to be influential, to define circumstances, to provide guidance, to stimulate action and/or thought, and to legitimate subsequent activities by their following. In many cases, by virtue of their role in one setting, they may be influential in another.

2   C. Geertz, *Interpretation of Cultures* (New York, Basic Books, 1973); R. Linger, *Knowledge and Politics* (New York, Free Press, 1975).

3   M. Polanyi, The *Tacit Dimensions* (New York, Doubleday, 1966).

4   R. Hamrin, *Managing Growth in the 1980s* (New York, Praeger, 1980); H. Striner, *Regaining the Lead* (New York, Praeger, 1984).

5   Y. Dror, *Policy Making Under Adversity* (New Brunswick, NJ, Transaction Books, 1985).

6   A. Miller, *Prisoners of Childhood* (New York, Basic Books, 1981); W. Grubb and M. Lazerson, *Broken Promises: How Americans Fail Their Children* (New York, Basic Books, 1982).

7   R. Heilbroner, *An Inquiry into the Human Prospect* (New York, W. W. Norton and Co, 1980).

8   M. Konner, *The Tangled Wing* (New York, Holt, Rinehart and Winston, 1982).

9   W. Anderson, *To Govern Evolution* (Orlando, FL, Harcourt Brace Jovanovich, 1987).

10   R. Lamm, "Copernican polities", *The Futurist,* October 1983, pages 5-11;
      G. Hardin, *Naked Emperor* (Los Angeles, CA, William Kaufman, 1982);
      D. Meadows *et al, The Limits to Growth* (New York, Universe Books,
      1972).

11   D. Golman, *Vital Lies, Simple Truths* (New York, Simon and Schuster,
      1985).

12   R. May, *The Meaning of Anxiety* (revised edition, New York, Norton,
      1977).

13   D. Michael, "Reason's shadow: notes on the psychodynamics of
      obstruction", *Technological Forecasting and Social Change, 26,* 1984, pages
      149-153.

14   R. May, *Man's Search for Himself* (New York, Norton, 1953).

15   O. Friedrich, *The End of the World* (New York, Prager, 1986).

16   R. Devaney, "Chaotic bursts in nonlinear dynamic systems", *Science,* 16
      January 1987, pages 342-345; J. Gleick, *Chaos: Making a New Science* (New
      York, Viking, 1987).

17   I. Prigogine and I. Stengers, *Order Out of Chaos* (New York, Bantam, 1984).

18   Y. Dror, "Visionary political leadership: on improving a risky requisite",
      International Political Science Review, 9(1), 1988, pages 7-22; see also M. Edelman,
      Constructing the Political Spectacle, (Chicago, Chicago University Press, 1988)
      especially Chapter 3.

19   E. Becker, *The Denial of Death* (New York, Free Press, 1973).

20   D. Michael, "Too much of a good thing? Dilemmas of an information society",
      Technological Forecasting and Social Change, 25, 1984, pages 347-354.

21   D. Michael and W. Anderson, "Norms in conflict and confusion: six stories in
      search of an author", *Technological Forecasting and Social Change, 31,* 1987, pages
      107-115.

22   Polanyi, *op cit,* reference 3.

23   D. Michael, *On Learning—to Plan and Planning to Learn* (San Francisco, CA, Jossey-
      Bass, 1973).

24   R. Bellah *et al, Habits of the Heart* (Berkeley, CA, University of California Press,
      1985).

25   B. Tuchman, *A Distant Mirror* (New York, Alfred A. Knopf, 1978); W. B.
      Yeats, "The second coming".

26   R. May, *Freedom and Destiny* (New York, Norton, 1981), page 89.

SOME OBSERVATIONS WITH REGARD TO A MISSING ELEPHANT

I begin with a Sufi story we're all familiar with. It's the story of the blind persons and the elephant. Recall that persons who were blind were each coming up with a different definition of what was "out there," depending on what part of the elephant they were touching. Notice that the story depends on the fact that there is a storyteller who can see that there is an elephant, different parts of which the blind people are fumbling around with. What I'm going to propose is that today, the storyteller is blind. There is no elephant. The storyteller doesn't know what he or she is talking about.

Less metaphorically, I'll put it this way: What is happening to the human race, in the large, is too complex, too interconnected, and too dynamic to comprehend. There is no agreed-on interpretation that provides an enduring basis for coherent action based on an understanding of the enfolding context.

Take any subject that preoccupies us. Attend to all the factors that arguably might seriously affect its current condition, where it might go, what might be done about it, and how to go about doing so.

I'll take poverty as an example. Think of the variety of factors that connect with poverty. If one were attempting to comprehend the factors seriously affecting poverty, one would have to attend to at least technology, environment, greed, crime, drugs, family, media presentation, education, governments, market economy, information flows, ethics, ideology, personalities, and events. All of these and more infuse any topic that we pay attention to and try to do something about. But, clearly, we can't attend to all of these factors (and others) because each has its own complex mix of interdependencies to be attended to.

Poverty is one of an endless series of examples. What we're faced with, essentially, is the micro/macro question: how circumstances in the small affect circumstances in the large and how circumstances in the large affect circumstances in the small. And we don't know—chaos theory, "butterfly effects," and complex adaptive systems not withstanding—how the micro/macro interchange operates in specific human situations. And for reasons I shall come to, I don't think we can know. In effect, we don't comprehend— can't comprehend—the kind of beast that holds the parts together: in this example, how they're held together for the human condition we call poverty. There isn't any elephant there.

Having asserted this, let me emphasize that I'm in no sense belittling our daily efforts to engage issues like poverty or other aspects of the human condition. Rather, I hope to add a deeper appreciation of the existential challenge we face, the poignancy of our efforts, and the admiration they merit as we try to deal with our circumstances.

Indeed, it seems to me that if we could acknowledge that we don't know what we're talking about in the large when we try to deal with any of the human issues we face, that acknowledgement would have very significant implications for how we perceive ourselves as persons and how we conduct our activities intended to help the human condition, including ourselves. I'll come to those implications presently.

But first, I want to offer some observations in support of my proposal that we don't know what we're talking about in the large by describing six characteristics that seem to be the source of the storyteller's blindness.

One more prefatory remark follows: I intend my observations to be as non-judgmental as I can. I believe I am describing characteristics of the human world that simply are. I am trying to be an observer, not an evaluator. However, the very nature of my language and what I select from this complexity to emphasize convey values, hence judgments, often unknown to me.

Let me state the first of six contributors to our ignorance. We have too much and too little information to reach knowledgeable consensus and interpretation within the available time for action. More information in the social realm generally leads to more uncertainty, not less. Usually, more information tells us that we need still more information to interpret what information we do have, whether it pertains to toxic substances, ecological protection, economic projections, welfare policy, social impacts of global warming, or the consequences of changes in procedures for public or private decision making. Therefore, the time it takes to reach agreement on the interpretation increases. During that time, the information increases as well. We need more information to interpret the information we have, and on and on.

Among the growing amount of information is that which increases our doubt about the integrity, validity, and reliability of the information we do have. There is enough information, nevertheless, to generate multiple interpretations of that information, which then adds another layer of information and interpretation that's required to use that information. And more information often stimulates the creation of more options. As a result, still more information is generated, including more information about the information, and so on around and around the self-amplifying "information loop".

Add, too, that information feedback seldom arrives at the time when it is needed for comparison with other information. Usually, if it arrives at all, it is too late to adjust the action or interpretation close to the time that initiated the feedback in the first place. Think, for example, of all the federal fund allocations for current social projects that are pegged to census information that is several years old. Or how long it takes to accumulate the evidence (feedback) and navigate the procedures before a judicial decision is made with regard to damage done years earlier. Or think of corporate or government revelations that are exposed years after the fact, too late for timely rectification. So, the first ignorance generator is inadequate information to reach knowledgeable decisions in the finite amount of time available for taking action.

Second, there is no shared set of value priorities. We make much of the fact that we share values, and we always say, "well, basically humans want the same things." Perhaps they do, at a survival level, but, beyond that, there is not a shared set of priorities with regard to values across cultures and often, as in the United States, within cultures. The priorities change with circumstance, time, and engaged persons.

Here are some examples in which value priorities differ depending on the person/group and circumstance: short-term expedience versus long-term prudent behavior and vice versa, group identity versus individual identity, individual responsibility versus societal responsibility, freedom versus equality, local claims versus larger claims for commitment, universal rights versus local rights (that, in the name of local rights, repudiate universal rights, e.g. fundamentalisms), human rights versus national interests (e.g. economic competition or nationalist terrorism), public interest versus privacy (the encryption conflict about health information, whether private or not), first amendment limits (pornography, etc.), and the potential gain of new knowledge versus its potential social costs. Who sets the rules of the game, and who decides who decides? These are all issues in which the priority of values is in contention. There's no reliable set of priorities in place that can be used decisively to choose among actions toward larger issues.

A third contribution to this lack of comprehension is what has been called the *dilemma of context*. How much do you and/or I need to know to feel responsible for actions and interpretations? How many layers of understanding are necessary to have enough background to deal with the foreground? There are no agreed-on criteria or methodology for how deeply to probe. (I should have observed at the beginning of my enumeration that these six factors are interdependent, interactive.) So, for example, the question of how much context is necessary in a situation to decide what to do about that situation very much depends on what values are held by participants in that decision making. And that raises another intractable context question: Who are the legitimate participants in the decision making with regard to deciding what constitutes a sufficient context? And who says so?

Just to remind you, a few of the differing claims defining the appropriate context are the dramatis personae's motives, the world of the media, cultural differences in public interpretations and responses, political styles, and historical/ mythic memories.

Choose any issue that's important to you and ask how much information I/we need in order that you or I can say that I/we have adequate context for thought and action? This is an unresolved realm. It is unresolved for me as well in the very act of giving this talk.

A fourth item is that our spoken language, the language we hear, cannot adequately map the complexity that I'm talking about. Our language, because we hear it or we read it, is linear. So, one thought follows another. Our language cannot adequately engage multiple interacting factors simultaneously. (Some poetry can, but we haven't yet figured out how to use poetry for policy making or for resolving issues of context, value priorities, or the like. And, perhaps some forms of visual language can help because they can be simultaneously presented in three dimensions.) Our noun/ verb structure emphasizes items, events, and stasis (i.e., is-ness, e.g., we say "this is a microphone" rather than engaging it as a multitude of processes in time and space that we call *micro-phone*). Nor can our language adequately map, in our ongoing minds, the circularity of cause and effect producing causes, producing effects. Nor the sustaining of a system, as a system, by virtue of the built-in circular feedbacks that maintain boundary relationships. In other words, our spoken/written language doesn't allow us to talk about these complexities in ways that are inherently informative about the complexities. In fact, it compounds these complexities because it unavoidably distorts our efforts to perceive a world of simultaneous, multiple, circular processes.

The fifth contribution to our inability to know what we are talking about is that there is an increasing, and—given the other contributions—unavoidable absence of reliable boundaries. By boundaries, I mean boundaries that circumscribe turf, relationships, concepts, identity, property, gender, time, and more. Without boundaries, we can't make sense of anything. William James wrote of a boundaryless world as one of "blooming, buzzing confusion." Boundaries are how we discriminate and partition experience to create meaning in all those nonmaterial realms, not just turf.

But, what is happening in this world, for reasons I've been describing (and others as well), is that these boundaries and their reliability are increasingly eroded, disintegrated, and becoming more and more ambiguous. All systems, including social systems, require boundaries to be coherent systems. It's the feedback that is determined by those boundaries in the system that allows a system to be self-sustaining. If there are no boundaries and no feedback, there is no self-sustaining quality that we call a system or that in the old story was called an elephant.

All that I've been emphasizing reduces the agreed-on criteria for boundary-defining feedback. Here are some examples, just to remind you: boundaries that are claimed for political correctness, identity, public versus private,

intellectual property, biological ethics questions. All of these are blurred, ambiguous areas, taken very seriously, that nevertheless don't allow the kind of linguistically and behaviorally discriminating boundary defining I think necessary to begin to comprehend the incomprehensibility of the complexity that we humans live in.

The sixth contributor to our inability to know what we are talking about is the self-amplifying, unpredictable acting out of the shadow residing in each human: our instincts, our extra-rational responses. This situation could be considered a consequence of the other contributors to our ignorance— though each of them is also a consequence of all the others. (Or so I think.) To be sure, this acting out allows for more creativity, but, often, in this complex world, the shadow is also in the service of violence, oppression, selfishness, extreme positions of all stripes—that whole upwelling of the nonrational, the nonreasonable that is so increasingly characteristic of all the world, not just the United States.

There was a time—a long time—when this sort of shadow-driven acting out did not well up to the current degree. The elephant depends on constraints, on boundaries, to be an elephant. In the past, ritual, repression, and suppression served to constrain such acting out or to quash it entirely. One's social and economic survival depended on playing by many explicit and implicit rules (boundaries). (Think of the upwelling of violence after the collapse of the Soviet empire.)

These circumstances make human governance uniquely problematic. By governance, I mean those shared practices by which a society's members act reliably toward each other. Government is one such way such practices are established via laws and so on. Shared child socialization practices and formal religions are others. For the reasons I am proposing here, the processes of governance can only become less and less effective. This, in turn, increases unreliability and adds its own contributions to the incomprehensibility of it all.

So much for six "ignorance-maintaining" characteristics. Perhaps they are variations on one theme, and surely others could be added. But I hope these are enough to make a presumptive case that our daily activities are ineluctably embedded in a larger context of ignorance—that we don't know what we're talking about.

So, what to do, how to go about being engaged in a human world we don't understand—and, if I'm on to something—we won't understand? Here are eight ways I find helpful in responding to the fact of our ignorance. (In spite of writing assertively, I hope it's clear that I include myself among those who don't know what they're talking about!) These aren't in any particular order, though I think the sequence they are in adds a certain coherence.

The first is to recognize that given our neurology and our shaping through evolutionary processes, we are unavoidably seekers of meaning. Recognizing that we are seekers of meaning, we also need to recognize that unavoidably, we live in illusions: socially and biologically created, constructed worlds that are nevertheless personally necessary. And, this necessity can evoke the best and the worst in us, as the long history of "true believers" amply evidences. I'm not implying that we can live outside of these constraints, but we need to be self-conscious about the fact that we do live in illusions and that there is no way for humans to avoid this. So, each of us needs to be self-conscious about our deep need that there be an elephant or for someone to tell us there really is an elephant. (Lots of authors and publishers thrive on this yearning.)

Second, it seems essential to acknowledge vulnerability and finiteness, both ours and our projects'. This is because we will be unavoidably ignorant and uninformed about the outcomes—the consequences of the consequences—of what we do.

Third, as all the great spiritual traditions emphasize, seek to live in poverty. Not material poverty—rather be poor in pride and arrogance and in the conviction that I/we know what is right and wrong, what must be done, and how to do it. Nevertheless, we must act—not acting is also acting—regardless of our vulnerability and finiteness.

Thus, my fourth suggestion is that a person or a group act in the spirit of hope. Hope, not optimism. Here I draw on the insight of Rollo May. As he put it, optimism and pessimism are conditions of the stomach, of the gut. Their purpose is to make us feel good or bad. However, hope has to do with looking directly at the circumstances we're dealing with, at the challenges we must accept as finite and vulnerable beings and activities, and recognizing the limits of our very interpretation of what we're committing ourselves to, still go on because one hopes that one can make a difference in the face of all that stands in the way of making a difference.

Fifth, this means one acts according to what I've been calling "tentative commitment". Tentative commitment means you are willing to look at the situation carefully enough, to risk enough, to contribute enough effort, to hope enough, to undertake your project. And to recognize, given our vulnerability, our finiteness, and our fundamental ignorance, that we may well have it wrong. We may have to back off. We may have to change not only how we're doing it but whether we do it at all. And then do so! Tentative commitment becomes an essential individual and group condition for engaging a world where we don't know what we are talking about.

Suggestion six, then, is to be "context alert" as a moral and operational necessity. Among other things, this carries a very radical implication, given the current hype about the information society that promises to put us in touch with practically infinite amounts of information. However, if you are context alert, you can only be deeply understanding of very few matters, because it takes time and effort to dig and check and deal with other people who have different value priorities, contexts, boundaries, and so on. This means there are only a few things that you can be "up on" at any given time. But, this is a very serious, unsolved, indeed unformulated, challenge for effective participation in the democratic process—whatever that might mean.

Number seven is that one must be a learner/teacher, a wary guide in the wilderness. Be question askers all the time, not answer givers.

Number eight again echoes the great spiritual traditions (all of which recognize our essential ignorance): practise compassion. Given the circumstances I have described, facing life requires all the compassion we can bring to others and to ourselves. Be as self-conscious as possible, as much of the time as possible, and thereby recognize that we all live in illusion, we all live in ignorance, and we all search for and need meaning. We all need help facing that reality, and that help goes by the name of practising compassion.

The blind must care for the blind.

DONALD N. MICHAEL SELECTED BIBLIOGRAPHY

Essay Permissions

Leadership's Shadow: The Dilemma of Denial

Reprinted from *Futures, 23, 1*. Michael, Donald N. "Leadership's Shadow: The Dilemma of Denial", pp. 69-79. © (1991), with permission from Elsevier.

Forecasting and Planning in an Incoherent Context

Reprinted from *Technological Forecasting and Social Change, 36.1-2*. Michael, Donald N. "Forecasting and Planning in an Incoherent Context", pp.79-87. © (1989), with permission from Elsevier

Technology and the Management of Change from the Perspective of a Culture Context

Reprinted from *Technology Forecasting and Social Change*, 5.3. Michael, Donald N. "Technology and the Management of Change from the Perspective of a Culture Context", pp. 219-232. © (1973), with permission from Elsevier.

With Both Feet Planted Firmly in Mid-Air: Reflections on Thinking About the Future

Reprinted from *Futures, 17, 2*. Michael, Donald N. "With Both Feet Planted Firmly in Mid-Air: Reflections on Thinking About the Future", pp.94-103. © (1985), with permission from Elsevier.

Some Observations with Regard to the Missing Elephant

Michael, Donald N. *Journal of Humanistic Psychology, 40, 1*. pp. 8 - 16. © (2000). Reprinted by Permission of SAGE Publications.

Selected Articles

"Man Into Space: A Tool and Program for Research in the Social Sciences", *American Psychologist*, June 1957, 12, 6, pp. 324-328.

"Space Exploration and the Values of Man", *Space Journal*, September 1959, 2, 1, pp. 9-15.

"Social Impact of Space Activities", in *The United States In Space (Usia/Nasa* Seminar). Washington, D.C.: NASA Office of Scientific and Technical Information, 1963, pp. 39-46.

"Free Time: A New Imperative in our Society", *Vital Speeches Of The Day*, 1963, pp. 616-620.

"Inhibitors and Facilitators to the Acceptance of Educational Innovations", *Inventing Eduction For The Future*, Werner Hirsch (ed), Chapter 14, pp. 268-279, (- 1965).

"Some Speculations on the Social Impact of Technology", in *Technological Innovation And Society*, Dean Morse and Aaron W. Warner (eds.), New York: Columbia University Press, May 1966, pp. 118-154.

"The Impact of Cybernation", in *Technology In Western Civilization*, Vol. 2, Melvin Kranzberg and Carroll W. Pursell, Jr. (eds.), Madison, Wisconsin: University of Wisconsin Press, 1967, pp. 655-669.

"Technology and the Management of Change from the Perspective of a Culture Context", *Technological Forecasting And Social Change*, 5, 1973, pp. 219-232.

"Competence and Compassion in an Age of Uncertainty," *World Future Society Bulletin, XVII*, I, Jan.-Feb. 1983, pp. 1-6.

"Too Much of a Good Thing? Dilemmas of an Information Society," *Vital Speeches Of The Day*, L, 2, 1983, pp. 38-42.

"Reason's Shadow: Notes on the Psychodynamics of Obstruction," *Technological Forecasting And Social Change, XXVI*, 2, 1984, pp 149-153.

"The Futurist Tells Stories", *What I Have Learned: Thinking About The Future Then And Now*, M. Marien and L. Jennings (eds.), Westport, Conn., Greenwood Press, l987, pp. 74-86.

"On Thinking About the Future", (revised) *Journal Of Humanistic Psychology*, 29, 1, Winter 1989, pp. 37-53.

"Six Stories In Search of An Author " (revised) with Anderson, W T., *Journal Of Humanistic Psychology* 29,2, Spring 1989, pp.145-166.

"Barriers and Bridges to Learning in a Turbulent Human Environment", *Barriers And Bridges To The Renewal Of Ecosystems And Institutions*, Gunderson, L., Holling, C., Light, S., (eds.), New York, Columbia, 1995, pp. 461-485.

"Forward: 1996 Reflections", "Epilogue*", Learning To Plan--And Planning To Learn*, (second ed.), Alexandria, VA. Miles River Press 1997.

"Denial: Control's Dark Companion", *The Millennium Bug: The Year 2000 Computer Problem*. Wouters, A., et al (eds.), Acco, Leuven, Belgium, 1998, Chapter 6, pp.79- 89.

"Some Observations Regarding a Missing Elephant", Speech given at Saybrook Graduate School conferral of an honorary Doctorate in Humane Letters, San Francisco, 1998.

Selected Books

Cybernation: The Silent Conquest, Santa Barbara: Center for the Study of Democratic Institutions, February 1962.

The Next Generation: The Prospects Ahead For The Youth Of Today And Tomorrow, New York, Random House 1965.

The Unprepared Society: Planning For A Precarious Future, New York: Basic Books, Inc., 1968.

On Learning To Plan—And Planning To Learn: Social Psychological Aspects of Changing Toward Future-Responsive Societal Learning. San Francisco, Jossey-Bass, 1973. (See also Second Edition— Alexandria Virginia Miles, River Press, 1997—which includes a new Foreword and an amended epilogue referencing Pierre Wack and Shell's use of Scenario Planning.)

Note: A full bibliography of Donald N. Michael's writings and an inventory of his library is available for download from the websites of the International Futures Forum, www.internationalfuturesforum.com *and Triarchy Press,* www.triarchypress.com

Publishers

TRIARCHY Press is an independent publishing house that looks at how organisations work and how to make them work better—both internally and in relation to each other and their environment. We present challenging perspectives on organisations in short and pithy, but rigorously argued, books.

The name 'Triarchy' comes from our founder Gerard Fairtlough's theory that challenges the hegemony of hierarchy in organisations and puts forward two alternative ways of organising power and responsibility in order to get things done: heterarchy and responsible autonomy. Our publications offer a number of different but related approaches to organisational issues from the fields of systems thinking, innovation, cultural theory, complexity and leadership studies.

Our key partnership with IFF continues the practices of breaking with established norms and finding new responses to our surroundings: practices that are becoming increasingly important as our natural, economic and social systems become more volatile and unpredictable. These challenges require us to embrace the potential of change rather than retreat towards familiarity and stagnation, opening the door to intelligent and innovative preparation for the future. IFF's thinking and writing take significant steps towards this. This is our fifh IFF publication, following *Ten Things to Do in a Conceptual Emergency* by Graham Leicester and Maureen O'Hara, *Beyond Survival* by Graham Leicester, *Transformative Innovation in Education* by Graham Leicester, Keir Bloomer and Denis Stewart and *Economies of Life* by Bill Sharpe.

Please tell us what you think about the ideas in this book. Join the discussion at:

www.triarchypress.com/telluswhatyouthink

www.triarchypress.com
info@triarchypress.com

Donald N. Michael

Don Michael (1923 – 2000) came to San Francisco in 1981 after retiring from his joint position as Professor of Planning and Public Policy and Professor of Psychology at the University of Michigan. Previously, he had worked for many years in policy circles in Washington, after gaining degrees in physics and in social psychology from Harvard University and in sociology from the University of Chicago.

James Crowfoot, a former colleague at the University of Michigan, wrote of him:

> *'Throughout his career, [he] focused on a wide range of emerging societal problems and the usefulness and limitations of scientific knowledge in responding to these problems... In the final years of his life, he focused on the complexity and uncertainty associated with the increasing scale and intensity of interacting impacts of human systems and biophysical systems and on the latest research on human functioning. His final work and writing as he described it focused on: "(1) the function of myth systems in social change, especially how beliefs about human nature affect personal, organizational and societal change and (2) understanding better the role of unconscious needs and motives (genetically and culturally sourced) in the behaviour of leaders, decision makers and organization members and their interplay with the social construction of reality." '*

Don was a remarkable person; his genius was in blending an astonishing intellect with a deeply compassionate soul and almost childlike delight and curiosity about the world and the sense we make of it. His humanity integrity, and commitment to confronting the most vexing and complex problems using wisdom that might stretch from cybernetics to Zen without trivializing either, continue to inspire and challenge everyone who knew him.

Graham Leicester is Director of the International Futures Forum.

International Futures Forum

INTERNATIONAL Futures Forum (IFF) is a non-profit organisation established to support a transformative response to complex and confounding challenges and to restore the capacity for effective action in today's powerful times.

At the heart of IFF is a deeply informed inter-disciplinary and international network of individuals from a range of backgrounds covering a wide range of diverse perspectives, countries and disciplines. The group meets as a learning community as often as possible, including in plenary session. And it seeks to apply its learning in practice.

IFF takes on complex, messy, seemingly intractable issues—notably in the arenas of health, learning, governance and enterprise—where paradox, ambiguity and complexity characterise the landscape, where rapid change means yesterday's solution no longer works, where long term needs require a long term logic and where only genuine innovation has any chance of success.